American Green

Class, Crisis, and the Deployment of Nature in Central Park, Yosemite, and Yellowstone

Stephen Germic

LEXINGTON BOOKS
Lanham • Boulder • New York • Oxford

LEXINGTON BOOKS

Published in the United States of America
by Lexington Books
4720 Boston Way, Lanham, Maryland 20706

12 Hid's Copse Road
Cumnor Hill, Oxford OX2 9JJ, England

British Library Cataloguing in Publication Information Available

Library of Congress Cataloging-in-Publication Data

Germic, Stephen, 1967–
    American green: class, crisis, and the deployment of nature in Central Park, Yosemite, and
Yellowstone / Stephen Germic.
        p. cm.
    Includes bibliographical references (p.).
    ISBN 0-7391-0228-1 (cloth: alk. paper)—ISBN 0-7391-0229-X (pbk.: alk. paper)
    1. National characteristics, American—Case studies. 2. United States—Social conditions—
19th century—Case studies. 3. Social classes—United States—History—19th century—Case
studies. 4. United States—Economic conditions—19th century—Case studies. 5. Financial
crises—Social aspects—United States—History—19th century. 6. Central Park (New York,
N.Y.)—History—19th century. 7. Yosemite National Park (Calif.)—History—19th century.
8. Yellowstone National Park—History—19th century. 9. Public spaces—Social aspects—United
States—History—19th century. 10. Nature—Social aspects—United States—History—19th
century. I. Title.
E169.1 .G458 2001
333.78'3'097309034—dc21   00-052030

Printed in the United States of America

♾™ The paper used in this publication meets the minimum requirements of American National
Standard for Information Sciences—Permanence of Paper for Printed Library Materials,
ANSI/NISO Z39.48–1992.

For Catherine and Eloise

Contents

Acknowledgments

Many people have devoted their skills, knowledge, and hard work to this project. I cannot overstate my gratitude to Kathryne V. Lindberg. She has dedicated enormous time, energy, and intelligence to this work and with a faith that has often exceeded my own. To Michael Stancliff's friendship, patience, and acute insightfulness I owe a very great deal indeed. Kevin Floyd and Sheila Lloyd have both read significant portions of this work and provided excellent advice. I would also like to thank Henry Golemba, Doug Noverr, Donald Pease, Ross Pudaloff, and Priscilla Wald. At Rowman & Littlefield Jason Hallman, Serena Leigh, Ginger Strader, and John Calderone deserve many thanks. I have Catherine and Eloise to thank most of all.

Introduction

The Geography of Exceptionalism

Those who live in any place . . . who have pretensions to create an institutionalized locus of social and political power, have to find or invent an imaginary sufficient to achieve some level of social cohesion, solidarity, and institutional order.
> —David Harvey, "From Space to Place and Back Again"

Parks are cultural and state institutions. They are also generally considered "natural" places, variously recreational and conservationist. Yet as parks—with strict boundaries, internal regulations, assigned budgets and personnel—they embody the tremendous difficulty of distinguishing the natural from the cultural. Most parks, in fact, are "contrived" nature; they are designated as natural and either physically or experientially constructed as such by particular people and institutions for nominal, if diverse, reasons.[1] If debate persists, seemingly ad infinitum, on the criteria for distinguishing the natural from the cultural, then parks, I venture, are places where the distinction fails absolutely.[2]

The following is both a theorization and a description of the complicated interests and factors that led to the creation of America's first parks, both urban and "wilderness." My central thesis is that the first parks deployed Nature to mitigate and even to resolve the most threatening social and economic crises in the nineteenth century outside of the Civil War. I am concerned to analyze and to disclose the relationship between the constructed Nature of America's first parks and the capitalist state, and, inseparably, such Nature and nationalism. I analyze and describe the manner by which America's first parks preserved not "nature," but the economic viability of the nation. Polemically, I assert, the fundamental function of American parks in the nineteenth century was economic and political, where politics refers to the discourse and activities of creating and maintaining a national consensus on certain decisive matters. Foremost among such matters is that of identity. Central to my argument is the fact that the organization and control of "natural" space, inseparable from its function as a capitalist instrument, has been vital to the constitution of American national identity.

Which is to say that the "geographies of exclusion"[3] America's first parks manifest not only define, constitute, and segregate social groups, but function to "purify" a national(ist) self. In the following I contend that the permanent fixture of class difference in nineteenth-century America made *class* the foundational category from which other differences, particularly racial differences, were *spatially* elaborated. But, crucially, while class difference was permanent, the actual constituency of particular classes was remarkably unstable, as, necessarily, were the socially vilified and/or economically exploited populations. This meant that if the ideal, necessarily and exclusively incorporated American self (blending the individual body with the "body" of the nation) was founded on class—where hegemony and privilege organized the factors of incorporation—and if the actual bodies who composed the privileged class were constantly in flux, then identity was radically ambiguous. My final and most broad contention is that an idealized concept of Nature was a principal "resource" exploited to manufacture the geographies of difference intended to mediate capitalist crises and stabilize and secure an idealized, which is to say unambiguous, yet abject, national identity.[4]

As the above should indicate, my use of the term "class" in what follows is decidedly complicated. The modern sense of class, referring to levels of social division based on economics and privilege, itself arose between 1770 and 1840 and, despite my later focus, is roughly a product of the industrial period with which I am concerned.[5] Furthermore, class is an important term in the field of natural history where it (along with species and genus) presumes to describe stable, strictly delimited, and essential orders of living things. This second use is rather opposed to the first by its derivation from a belief in immutable *natural* laws, while, as Raymond Williams writes, the "essential history of the introduction of *class*, as a word that would supercede older names for social divisions, relates to the increasing consciousness that social position is made rather than merely inherited."[6] According to Williams the "scientific" use of the term precedes the social by approximately a century. The widespread use of "class" among reformers and apologists for the new industrial system in the nineteenth century represents an attempt to carry the understood stability of the scientific term to the social arena, where it could function both rhetorically and epistemologically to relieve anxieties about a constantly "revolutionizing" capitalist society. Thus, the social use of the term implies both some nostalgia for a certain preindustrial social order and an attempt to use a partly scientific concept to reassert some of the comfort associated with that order during a period of remarkable social instability.

Of course, according to the ideological demands of the American social and economic structure in the nineteenth century, class must necessarily both function and disappear. When, by the mid-nineteenth century, race becomes the privileged term of social difference, a categorical sliding, has, to a large degree, occurred. My use of "class" is intended primarily to mark a constant social difference among groups that may themselves be internally highly variable, especially as race comes to replace class as a category intended to maintain social hierarchy. Insofar as class is itself a term intended to impose stable social distinction my use is also, at some level, inevitably ironic, though functionally descriptive.

Also important to understanding my argument is a clear idea of what I mean by "American exceptionalism"—a term I employ frequently in what follows. There are two conventional understandings of American exceptionalism which are themselves closely related. The first, itself derived from two main traditions, is familiar to literary and cultural historians. It extends from a Columbian era rhetoric of America as a place of possibility and paradise through a Puritanical notion of mission, where America represents a nation of ideal politics and virtue, a "model" for other nations. One historian, Henri Baudet, has written on the Columbian era idea of America as a paradise that the new continent became a place, "onto which all identification and interpretation, all dissatisfaction and desire, all nostalgia and idealism seeking expression could be projected."[7] Sir Thomas More's *Utopia*, which draws heavily from Amerigo Vespucci's account of travels to the New World, is, of course, the most famous articulation from a European perspective of the imaginative possibilities America offered.[8] In More's work America becomes the place where all the problems that plague European nations (including plagues and class conflicts) are either resolved or simply never develop.[9]

More's *Utopia*, which was intended, according to its author, as an "example for correction [of European] errors," foreshadowed the Puritanical inflection of American exceptionalism.[10] Recently historian Jack P. Greene has written that the colony at Massachusetts Bay was the "most ambitious . . . attempt by English Puritans to establish a redemptive community of God's chosen people" in the New World.[11] The multiply inflected idea of "redemption" and its relation to American exceptionalism is taken up at the end of chapter 2; here I will introduce the second principal notion of exceptionalism before returning to the Puritans, at which point I will discuss John Winthrop's early articulation of the two concepts' interrelations.

The second notion of exceptionalism, more familiar to labor historians, was introduced by Werner Sombart in 1906 with his book, *Why Is There No Socialism in the United States?* According to Sombart, America is "exceptional" because, unlike European industrialized nations, it has never harbored an influential socialist or even working-class movement.[12] During the 1950s and 60s political commentators began looking back to Sombart and building on Alexis de Tocqueville's comment in *Democracy in America* that "the position of Americans," according to Tocqueville's understanding of western political systems and peoples, was "quite exceptional."[13] As an exception to the rule the United States is characterized by the general absence of both class consciousness and effective and organized resistence to capitalism. I do not exactly concur with Sombart and other exceptionalist historians about the radical history of the United States; along with many New Labor historians I think there is ample evidence of the insurgence of militant labor, especially in the nineteenth century. At the same time the record suggests clearly that radicalism has failed; capitalism has prospered and continues to prosper, and class differences both remain and widen, nationally and globally.

It is possible to discover the close relation of these two notions of exceptionalism (one emphasizing natural bounty and political idealism, the other emphasizing the supposed absence of class revolution) as early as John Winthrop's speech aboard the *Arabella* in 1630. The speech begins with an obviously anxious assertion of the need to preserve social differences along the lines of class division in the New World: "God Almightie in his most holy and wise providence hath soe disposed of the Condicion of mankinde, as in all times some must be rich some poore, some high and eminent in power and dignitie; others mean and in subjection."[14] Winthrop seeks to preserve an essentially monarchial social order, fully aware that its literal existence will be a conspicuous absence in America. With no royal figure to mediate God's divine plan in the New World, Winthrop skillfully confuses divine ordinance and class division: "All men being thus (by divine providence) ranked into two sortes, rich and poore; under the first are comprehended all such as are able to live comfortable by their own means duly improved; all others are poore according to the former distribution." Winthrop's anxiety about the poor rising up and "shaking off their yoake," reveals that the understanding of class difference as *socially* constituted may have been operative before the proper rise of industrialism, as Raymond Williams suggests. It is precisely such a social understanding that Winthrop seeks to suppress; he would have it take the form of a transcendent edict. It is in this sense that class, or more exactly, a particular knowledge or understanding of class, one that might motivate revolutionary ideas, "disappears," or is obscured by the ideological machinations of American exceptionalism.

At the height of American industrialization and geographic expansion in the later nineteenth century, the enormous complexity of the American social scene foreclosed any appeal to divinity for the maintenance of social order. And yet, according to the demands of the capitalist system, a social order based on class difference still somehow had to be maintained. The problem confronting American social and economic leaders was still, as with Winthrop, that of potential democracy. The deep and manifold economic crises attendant to American industrialization and expansion, when a heterogenous mass of workers and potential workers had relatively simple access to radical ideas and organizations, pressed American ideological operators and processes to find ways to compel "the people" to serve transcendent interests. Such a compelling need was especially marked amid episodes of economic and financial crisis.

"Crisis" and "panic" are multivalent terms I employ recurrently in the following. One hears or reads of economic crises and financial panics, and, with equal or greater frequency, one sees the terms applied to individual emotional and psychic conditions. I preserve and simultaneously exploit the manifold meanings of these terms, though I do so while also regarding the use of terminology within the discourses of economics and psychology whenever possible, or whenever some definitional consensus is available. "Panic" as a metaphor for economic crisis is decidedly apt, suggesting as it does a profound insecurity. During periods of economic crisis latent national and personal insecurities are made manifest and exaggerated. The socially constituted institutions that provide security, including banks, but also cultural institutions and even materially built environments, are thrown into disarray by panic. These are institutions with firm boundaries that function to organize personal identity. The fact that one goes from the bank to the opera to the uptown restaurant or apartment greatly reflects *and* determines one's social meaning and privilege. If such a network is disrupted, then the identity it inscribes is likewise disrupted, to a greater or lesser degree, depending on the points in the network that cease to function according to expectations. Necessarily, the bank is a foundational point in the network of the institutions and identities of a capitalist society. When the bank becomes a site of panic, general categoric disarray ensues.

The origins of financial crises have been various, and they include such momentous events as wars, natural disasters (and natural "bounties" [or agricultural overproduction]), and political disruptions. According to economist Hyman Minsky, such events precipitate a "displacement" of the macroeconomic system.[15] Such a displacement alters the economic outlook of financial actors and institutions "by changing profit opportunities in at least one important sector of the economy."[16] Consequently, as investment patterns shift, some sectors become depleted of capital while others become overvalued. In these latter sectors a "boom" often occurs. The foundation of a boom—credit and speculation, including the swelling of the total money supply—is notoriously unstable. Economist Charles P. Kindleberger writes: "Prices increase, giving rise to new profit opportunities and attracting still further firms and investors. Positive feedback develops, as new investment leads to increases in income that stimulate further investment and further income increases."[17] The overvaluing that ensues rests on the overestimation of prospective returns among investors, while the foundational instability arises from low cash availability and requirements. Credit is extended on the euphoric or imagined promise of returns (if the returns were actual, the influx of cash would greatly stabilize the situation). Kindleberger elaborates the fragility of such a situation:

> [Individuals and firms buy] on margin, or by installments, under circumstances in which one can sell the asset and transfer with it the obligation to make future payments. . . . When the number of firms and households indulging in these practices grows large . . . speculation for profits leads away from normal, rational behavior to what have been described as "manias" or "bubbles." The word "mania" emphasizes the irrationality; "bubble" foreshadows the bursting.[18]

Financial crisis thus primarily describes a condition of extreme excess of value in a major sector of the economy. When the bubble bursts, or when the supply of credit can no longer be extended on the promise of profits from receipts, panic follows. Creditors call in notes, investors go to redeem stock, and the absence of cash reserves reveals the irrationality—which might better be described as the immateriality—of the "boom." With this knowledge, panic is likely to increase. Kindleberger's analysis of financial mania and panic is especially relevant not simply because it endures as an influential theory of financial crisis,[19] but because Kindleberger has tested the model at length against the conditions of the Panic of 1873, which crucially involved the nineteenth-century railroad baron Jay Cooke and, as I advance and emphasize further in chapters 3 and 4, Yellowstone National Park.

According to Kindleberger, the Panic of 1873 is distinguished by its international character and by the multiplicity of economic "displacements" that led to manic financial behavior.[20] The Franco-Prussian War (1870-71) and the Prussian War against Austria (1866-69) were prime factors in the European depression of the period. European investors moved enormous capital, roughly $1 billion, to the recovering U.S. economy between 1865 and June 1873. The greater part of this investment went into U.S. government bonds, and the government used the majority of this income to subsidize railroad expansion. Railroads were *the bubble market* of the second half of the nineteenth century. The mania of railroad investment and track production soured instantly to a panic when Jay Cooke & Co., the chief financial liability of which was the Northern Pacific Railroad, closed its doors to trading on 18 September 1873. I submit in the following that overvaluation and overproduction in economic and financial sectors, and railroads in particular, had everything to do with the financial and cultural investment in the *production* of Nature in America's first parks.

In episodes of severe crisis the fundamental distinction (and indispensable contradiction) of capitalist society is threatened: class difference. It often becomes (violently) obvious that the workers, or less privileged, may assume command of the political machine and means of production. The two great panics in the United States of the second half of the nineteenth century had spatial causes related to continental overexpansion and the devaluation of the urban built environment—representative spatial contradictions of capitalism. America's first parks represent the "spatial fix," as geographer David Harvey employs the term,[21] to various, and especially spatial, contradictions that plague a capitalist social and economic system. Furthermore, the parks' economic function was inseparable from their social function of reasserting the secure distinctions of class and race, while at the same time clouding, through a symbolic constitution of American identity, such differences.

The focus of chapter 1 is on America's first great urban park, New York's Central Park, and its designer, Frederick Law Olmsted. Central Park, I argue, was a "natural" *place* that functioned at once to produce or maintain *and* reveal social distinctions.[22] The park arose, not coincidentally, during a period of severe economic crisis, namely, the Panic of 1857. In chapter 2 I focus on Olmsted himself, besides his direct role in the formation of the park because he, as I will show, so clearly experienced an emotional crisis, or panic, related to insecurities about his own personal and social identity. I suggest that his personal anxieties had social and economic origins and that these inevitably influenced his vision and construction of public spaces in the United States, including not only Central Park, but Yosemite, where he acted as the first park commissioner in 1864.

Chapters 3 and 4 examine Yellowstone and the events that led up to, and somewhat following, its declaration as a national park in 1872. A particular goal of these chapters is to ascribe capitalist agency to the manufacture of a "natural" public place in highly contested territory of the American West; therefore I discuss Jay Cooke, owner and principal financial promoter of the Northern Pacific Railroad that would come to service the Yellowstone region and the park. While many deserve or have tried to take credit for coming up with the idea of a national park, Cooke acted on the notion and funded the promotional events, including explorations and lectures, that led directly to the 1872 establishment of the park.

In chapters 3 and 4 I apply the notion of spatial production first advanced by the influential spatial theorist Henri Lefebvre to Yellowstone and the complex dynamics of continental expansion in the northern plains and Rockies. As I elaborate in chapter 3, "the production of space" refers to the literal and abstract manner by which physical territory is incorporated into a capitalist system and achieves both symbolic and exchange value. Yellowstone is a particularly apt arena for this discussion because it first entered "American consciousness" as a kind of sublime, and therefore inevitably symbolic, place during the fur-trapping era of the early nineteenth century. The physical features of the region begat "tall tales" and, equally, incredulity. These tales inspired later nineteenth-century explorations (beginning in 1860) but, curiously, less emphasis was given by explorers to the awesome reality of Yellowstone than to its peaceful or picturesque characteristics.[23] Which is not to say that the explorers were describing actual or unmediated physical features, but rather the culturally constituted response to such features.

Elizabeth McKinsey, in *Niagara Falls: Icon of the American Sublime*, identifies a moment at which the sublime tends to disappear as a characteristic emotional response to "dramatic" American scenery: "Changes in the image of Niagara Falls after about 1860 indicate a profound shift in attitude toward nature. Both the actual scenes at the Falls and the aesthetic assumptions of artists who journeyed there reveal the eclipse of the sublime as a motive force in American culture."[24] I would assert that the eclipse of the sublime is due to the ideological overdetermination of "nature" as Nature, or landscape. Examining the descriptions of Yellowstone explorers in the later nineteenth century reveals that travelers were rarely filled with awe and terror before the face of "nature" (though, as I show, this response does not completely disappear); more likely, they were calmed by placid and organized vistas. In fact, climbing mountains to view the landscape was a means of constituting the territory as a kind of landscape painting, complete with the visual rhetoric and tropes of the American landscape tradition. In particular, constituting the contested territory of the region as landscape effectively erased the history of Native presence, including the ongoing conflict in which the explorers were engaged. This "erasure" is an important aspect of the ideological perspective I am referring to when I discuss the deeply related notions of landscape, the picturesque and, finally, Nature.[25]

Elaborating the economic background of Yellowstone National Park, including its role in precipitating, resolving, and obscuring economic crisis, discloses the economic origins of the production of Nature that is central to the ideology of American exceptionalism. According to the usage I have already established, American exceptionalism concerns the double maintenance and obfuscation of class difference. American exceptionalism is also, and quite relatedly, about motivating and justifying United States imperialism. Imperialism is part of capitalism's "spatial fix," and, as the "production of space," had a fundamental connection to crises of production (in fact, overproduction) in urban and industrial centers. The ideological elaboration of the West as Nature, or landscape, is intended, in large part and in manifold ways (through the promotion of emigration or railroad employment of surplus labor, or rhetorically promising infinite resources) to resolve threatening class tensions located principally, though not exclusively, in urban areas.

I am also concerned with the role of Yellowstone Park in manufacturing geographies of exclusion. On the one hand, the reservation of "nature" required and facilitated reservations for various Native nations. People who lived in the area of the park were either killed or interned elsewhere attendant to the park's establishment, a fact that the notion of public recreation functions to obscure. This is the park's most obvious manifestation of a geography of exclusion and it suggests one manner by which Nature functions to transform class difference into racial difference; though, in this case, the transformation is rather indirect. On the other hand, the park was constituted as a national *symbolic place* that not only functioned spatially to organize social relations but to constitute an idealized, or, more exactly, exceptionalized American identity. Lauren Berlant has asserted that the "national symbolic" refers to "the order of discursive practices whose reign within a national space produces, and also refers to, the 'law' in which the accident of birth within a geographic/political boundary transforms individuals into subject of a collectively held history."[26] I adopt this notion while emphasizing the role of place rather than narrative, to which place may be closely connected but not obviously inscribed. As a national symbolic place, Yellowstone was perceived as a representation of national ideals and national self-image: a grand landscape painting that stood as a metaphor for America itself. As such, the subjective experience of the park ideally functioned as a ritual of incorporation, melding the body of the "American" with the body of "America." That is, true to the ideology of American exceptionalism, the park both "erased" differences (and the violence of physically imposing spatial differentiation), especially the dynamically confused categories of race and class, and maintained them.

Chapter One

Capital Contradictions: Frederick Law Olmsted and the Labor of Culture

> Ten thousand vehicles careering through the Park this perfect after-
> noon. Such a show! . . . Private barouches, cabs and coupes . . . the full
> oceanic tide of New York's wealthy and "gentility.". . . I suppose, as
> a proof of limitless wealth, leisure, and the aforesaid "gentility," it was
> tremendous. Yet what I saw those hours . . . confirms a thought that
> haunts me every additional glimpse I get of our top-loftical general or
> rather exceptional phases of wealth and fashion in this coun-
> try—namely, that they are ill at ease.
>
> —Walt Whitman, "Specimen Days"[1]

> It avails not, neither distance nor space—
> distance avails not.
>
> —Walt Whitman, "Crossing Brooklyn Ferry"

According to Whitman above, the wealthy Central Park paraders are "ill at ease" because they are "too conscious, cased in too many cremements." Some of their faces, he writes, are "corpse-like, so ashy and listless." This masking, or falseness, equated rather abruptly by Whitman with death, is highlighted by its appearance after a passage describing a Park policeman with whom Whitman frequently engages in conversation. This man, "a well-form'd sandy complexion'd young fellow," Whitman tells us at some length, enjoys his job, in large part because it allows him to "see life."[2] The pay, according to Whitman, is adequate ($2.40 a day), but for the officer the excitement of experiencing "real life" is his job's greatest reward.

Whitman rarely attempted to disguise the erotic terms of his encounters and he makes no such effort in the instance above. This absence of masking is in keeping with the class-based distinctions, between reality and falseness, life and death, Whitman is formulating. The wealthy encase themselves, in carriages and makeup, such that, even in a "natural" space, they smell not of "grass and woods and shores," but, "of soaps and essences, very rare maybe, but suggesting the barber-shop—something that turns stale and musty in a few hours anyhow."[3]

While parading through a "natural" space the wealthy bear only a negative relation to "nature," while the policeman's relation is unconsciously direct, as suggested by Whitman's adjective, "sandy," which metonymically associates the policeman with the "shores." Whitman is here expressing one form, albeit complexly layered, of a broad cultural concern about the distinction of "barbarism" (evidenced by "wild" or atavistic natural associations) and "civilization" in the nineteenth century. Furthermore, he is disclosing a crucial insight into the complex role of Nature as a constructed place in the elaboration of such social distinctions. Central Park was apparently made for the wealthy, as Whitman suggests when he explains the actual duties of the officer: stopping runaway "nags," keeping "roughs . . . 'off the grass.'"[4] By parading in a multiply "masked" fashion, the wealthy announce their difference from rough nature and their degree of civilization through their identification with idealized Nature. In Central Park, where a rugged geography had been greatly transformed and rebuilt as a massive landscape garden, the ablutions of the wealthy are reflected back to them. In Nature, they see themselves.

In Central Park geography was a territorial and discursive resource exploited to manufacture and to obscure social differentiations, differentiations based principally on the at once precarious and firm fact of class difference—precarious, because amid the unstable transitions of capitalism the constituency of the hegemonic class was itself unstable, and firm because class difference itself withstood such instabilities remarkably well. Though, I should emphasize and as I will demonstrate, the Park was, in various ways, advertised, announced, and rhetorically expounded as a place conducive to the refinement and elevation of the "masses." It was promoted as a species of cultural institution that would universalize and incorporate threatening differences in urban space. The refined Nature of the Park was to act as both a mirror and a model, at once reassuring identity and presenting an ideal, complete with manicure and evoking placidity, toward which a massive constituency of working and often protesting poor were intended to fashion themselves.

Yet besides being productive of distinction, Central Park was economically productive. The diverse and critical economic efficacy of Central Park, its role in mediating national crises attendant to the Panic of 1857 and the following depression, can only be properly evaluated when placed in the context of broader social crises, capitalist contradictions, and deeply embedded paradoxes of representational, republican politics. I approach these issues primarily through an examination of Central Park's principal designer, and, in its first years, manager: Frederick Law Olmsted. After decades languishing in relative obscurity, known mostly to urban historians and professional landscape architects, Frederick Law Olmsted has recently emerged to extraordinary popular acclaim. A good deal of his voluminous writings have been edited and released, in more than six volumes; four books devoted to his life and works have appeared in the last five years; there have been numerous newspaper, magazine, and journal articles; and, the Society for the Preservation of Olmsted Parks was formed in 1987. In fact, Olmsted's home in Brookline, Massachusetts, was recently included in the system of national historic parks.

That Olmsted deserves the attention is indisputable. If not always fully responsible, he played a major role in the creation of two of the most celebrated public spaces in the United States—New York's Central Park and Yosemite National Park—and he was the prominent designer of countless other parks and institutions across North America, including Prospect Park, parks in Montreal, Boston, Buffalo, and Detroit; residential communities in Atlanta, Long Island, and Chicago; the grounds of the Columbian Exposition of 1893; and universities, including UC Berkeley and Stanford. Olmsted has been hailed, rightly, I submit, as the single most influential designer of public space in North American history.[5]

Whether or not we are always aware of it, we are all familiar with Olmsted's work. It is very likely that we are also extremely thankful for it, though it is precisely this grateful attitude that has discouraged critical scrutiny of Olmsted that may violate the grain of his own visual and verbal explanation and elaboration of his productions. Olmsted has had his critics—especially among his contemporaries—but such have been largely silenced by the legion of critics and scholars devoted to a veneration of his accomplishments. His importance as an intellectual, that is, as a mediating figure and designer of mediating spaces for nineteenth-century social, political, and economic crises should be abundantly clear in what follows, and though both he and his designs have been attracting greater attention, Olmsted's influence in the race and class politics of the latter half of the nineteenth century remains woefully underscrutinized by scholars of American public space.

1.

Capitalism is characterized by contradiction. For example, it is well known that individual capitalists tend to act in ways that run against the interests of capital in general or the interests of capitalists taken as a whole. A primary symptom of this contradiction is the *overaccumulation* that occurs as capitalists in competition with one another seek to produce the greatest amount of goods (and profit) with the greatest efficiency and least cost. As Hegel, one of the earliest theorists of overproduction, states tersely in *The Philosophy of Right*, "the evil consists precisely in an excess of production and in the lack of a proportionate number of consumers."[6] David Harvey has recently commented on the problem: "too much capital is produced in aggregate relative to the opportunities to employ that capital."[7] Harvey points further that overaccumulation may manifest itself in several ways, including the overproduction of commodities, falling rates of profit, and surplus capital—idle production centers and money without good investment opportunity.[8] The theorist Georges Bataille has termed such overaccumulation "the accursed share." Bataille suggests, drawing an organic metaphor, the "excess energy (wealth) can be used for the growth of a system . . . [but] if the system can no longer grow, or if the excess cannot be completely absorbed in its growth, it must necessarily be lost without profit; it must be spent, willingly or not, gloriously or catastrophically."[9] Bataille might say it is spent on cultural monuments or on war; certainly, it is often both.

In the United States in 1856 overaccumulation was considerable. Historian Franklin Folsom, analyzing the Panic of 1857, writes that a "hectic boom had followed the depression of 1854-1855. In the United States it had consisted of a vast expansion of railroads, new industries, and new cities. But there were soon more transportation and more production than the country could absorb."[10] Generally attendant to overaccumulation is the problem of surplus labor. In the later nineteenth century in particular, massive labor-dependent industry relied on processes like the mechanization of agriculture, the recruitment of female and child labor, and immigration to provide a steady supply of surplus labor that guaranteed depressed wages (and, evidencing contradiction, depressed consumption).[11] However, in the process of building an industrial landscape that could absorb so many workers, capitalism, through the continual reinvestment of surplus value, created a fixed environment that, almost immediately, became a liability if not an outright Achilles' heel. The immobile landscape of production manifested an urban environment rife with unemployed workers and widespread poverty. This situation naturally contributed to labor organization and worker radicalization—the bane of capitalism.

What needs to be emphasized, decidedly, is the degree to which the problems confronting the interests of capital in the nineteenth century were spatial problems. The "spatial" factor has been a pressing but problematic and largely underdeveloped aspect of radical social analysis, though both Hegel and Marx after him recognized the significance of the spatial component of social and economic relations. In fact, Hegel proposed, in *The Philosophy of Right*, one of the most fundamental questions for Marx. As Hegel introduced it, "When the masses begin to decline into poverty," they can either be maintained by the wealthier classes, "or they might be given subsistence indirectly through being given work."[12] But the latter solution is not seriously entertained, because, as I have already quoted, "the evil consists precisely in an excess of production": "It hence becomes apparent that despite an excess of wealth civil society is not rich enough, i.e. its own resources are insufficient to check excessive poverty and the creation of a penurious rabble. . . . This inner dialectic of civil society thus drives it . . . to push beyond its own limits and seek markets, and so its necessary means of subsistence, in other lands which are either deficient in the goods it has overproduced, or generally backward in industry, &c."[13]   *(Hegel as oracle)*

Can the crisis of overproduction and surplus labor be resolved through imperialist conquest? Hegel's teleological assertion in *The Philosophy of History* that "America is . . . the land of the future, where, in the ages that lie [ahead], the burden of the World's History shall reveal itself" is qualified by the observation that space must be exhausted before history's perfectability is actualized, that is, before time is made irrelevant: "North America is still in the condition of having land to begin to cultivate. Only when, as in Europe, the direct increase in agriculturists is checked, will the inhabitants, instead of pressing outwards to occupy the fields, press inwards upon each other . . . and so form a compact system of civil society and require an organized state."[14]

Hegel directs us to the especially speculative character of his geographical teleology by using what is at once a metaphor and a pun in his concluding remarks on the New World: "It is for America to abandon the ground [grund] on which hitherto the History of the World has developed itself."[15] America is to abandon such *ground*, that is, through "development"; the elegance of the formulation obscures the manifold obstacles confronting such development, like worker (not to mention aboriginal) resistance. Which is to say that Hegel's Idealist metaphor of a transcendent America finally refuses the economism which informed his notion that expansion could defuse proletarian unrest. If, as Hegel rightly suggests, capital hesitates to employ labor to defuse agitation because of already endemic overproduction, and instead turns to expansion, then *consumption* should be regarded as a principal goal and aspect of imperialism—consumption, that is, of surplus labor and capital. It is precisely in the economics of such consumption that the urban park is deeply related to imperialism: a massive project like Central Park at once consumes surplus capital and labor and is socially reproductive rather than materially productive. It consumes without market saturation and attendant devaluation and represents a direct investment in the restoration of value to the built environment.

Hegel's "penurious rabble" is, furthermore, in roughly Hegelian terms, that "element within civil society which negates its universal principle."[16] The class of victims of capitalist economic violence, who can feel no duty toward civil society, threatens the political foundation of the liberal, representative capitalist system. The "rabble" maintain the hard knowledge that they are not represented, that they have unserved particularist interests. In short, they may refuse and/or are structurally refused universalization. Urban reform movements and spatial reorganization, the environmental deployments of culture in the nineteenth century, were intended to effect the identification of the unrepresentable with the universal through a spatial and symbolic rhetoric. I will return to develop this important point after introducing the spatial and economic context in which Central Park was established.

From a perspective rooted in the dynamics and contradictions of the built environment, the Park is constructed because capital contends continuously with the physical landscape it produces. Capital needs to be mobile to create markets and extract resources, and at the same time it requires a solid infrastructure for production and consumption. In the built environment of the urban production center capital creates an immobile landscape of factories, housing districts, and consumption centers which invariably become decentered by capitalist expansion. This built environment cannot be abandoned without enormous loss, thus, in short, capital creates spatial barriers where before there were none; or, at the very least, it creates barriers on its own terms of scale and order.[17] As Harvey writes,

> Capital represents itself in the form of a physical landscape created in its own image, created as use values to enhance the progressive accumulation of capital. The geographical landscape that results is the crowning glory of past capitalist development. But at the same time it expresses the power of dead labor over living labor, and as such it imprisons and inhibits the accumulation process within a set of specific physical constraints.[18]

A crucial objective for the intellectuals and planners of capitalist development is figuring a way to maintain the value of the old built environment while, at the same time, opening up and exploring a fresh space for accumulation. This double function of spatial production was precisely the sort in which Frederick Law Olmsted was engaged.

Central Park served to decrease the volatility of urban space. It was not only that the visual and spatial rhetoric of the Park deployed "strategies of persuasive imaging [and thus] maintained a specific reading of history and reinforced the ideology of expansion," as Patricia Hills maintains of Western landscape art in the nineteenth century.[19] This, as I will show, Olmsted's design for Central Park certainly did, but, additionally, Central Park was a public works project in the name of "nature" that helped to resolve multifaceted crises of spatial contradiction and overaccumulation through urban engineering, the expenditure of surplus capital, and the employment and/or "refinement" of the dangerous population of surplus laborers. While maintaining and elaborating a classic American rhetoric of infinitude and exceptionalism, Central Park mediated profoundly threatening municipal and national crises. Furthermore, as a cultural institution, the Park was a primary site, or "place," for subjective constitution according to the contradictory demands of representational politics. That is, according to a tradition of cultural discourse from Friedrich Schiller through Samuel Taylor Coleridge and Matthew Arnold, Central Park (and other parks and designs I introduce in the following) was formally and rhetorically (or in a pedagogical fashion) intended to effect the universalization of the category of "man," so as to incorporate, according to hegemonic terms and needs, the disparate, differentially interested, categorically resistant, and outright revolutionary "masses." As an institution of American exceptionalism, Central Park was intended to disabuse the masses of class interest, to obscure class difference, to repress class conflict and to interest them, in the name of disinterest, in interests other than their own. Finally, Olmsted's urban masterpiece, Central Park, materialized the nineteenth century's greatest abstraction and ideal: the nation. Olmsted intended the Park to re-create the individual, or the "mass" individual, who was, all too apparently, capable of at once violently dismantling and re-creating, on revolutionary terms, the state.

As I described in the introduction, "exceptionalism" refers in part to a series of rhetorical and symbolic forms inherited from the Puritanical notion of mission and from a Columbian era rhetoric of possibility and paradise. This combined tradition charters the sense of national destiny that made anything short of continental conquest inadmissable. The urban park, as a visual and spatial rhetoric of exceptionalism in the above sense, was, precisely, landscape art that functioned in the "persuasive" manner Hills describes above. The urban park represents the landscape as America, emptied of conflict and promising infinite resources; the territory of the American continent appears uncontested, or already within the Union. One of the points I elaborate in this chapter is that the above notion of exceptionalism is not distinct from the notion of exceptionalism as the absence of a radical and influential working class, but rather an aspect of it.[20]

2.

"Nature or Blood": this could well have been the standard of the indefatigable writer and "father" of landscape architecture,[21] Frederick Law Olmsted. An instructive episode, for the purpose of making apparent the relationship of Central Park to class conflict, occurred when construction of Central Park was ongoing during the panic of 1857. On his way to work as New York Central Park superintendent, Olmsted had to "penetrate a body of men estimated by some newspapers to be five thousand strong." He recollects:

> As I worked my way through the crowd, no one recognizing me, I saw and heard a man then a candidate for reelection as a local magistrate addressing it from a wagon. He urged that those before him had a right to live, he assumed that they could live only through wages to be paid by the city; and to obtain these he advised that they should demand employment of me. If I should be backward in yielding it—here he held up a rope and pointed to a tree, and the crowd cheered.[22] (*PFLO* III: 15)

Olmsted could not bring himself to name his possible fate. This denial may be some measure of the level of class violence, and certainly the fear of it, in the antebellum North. The unemployed who confronted him carried a banner that read "Bread or Blood." Indeed, the threat of urban rebellion was real. The record of actual violence and the rhetoric of violence which can be attributed to class difference before and around the panic of 1857 is quite remarkable.

As early as the mid-1830s President Jackson's actions against the Bank of the United States precipitated a retaliatory depression which set new precedents for worker and capitalist antagonisms in the United States. President of the Bank, Nicholas Biddle, felt that widespread "evidence of suffering" was necessary before Jackson would consider a Bank re-charter; he therefore initiated a "steady course of firm restriction" that did much to bring about such suffering.[23] Through the worker alliances that grew out of the crisis Ely Moore, president of the New York General Trades Union, became the first representative of organized labor in Congress.[24] In his first Congressional speech he threatened:

> Both the laws of God and man, justify resistance to the robber, and the

homicide, even unto death! They are considered necessary guards against the encroachments of mercenary ambition and tyranny, and the friends of exclusive privileges, therefore, may with propriety dread their power and influence. The union of the working men is not only a shield of defense against hostile combinations, but also a weapon of attack that will be successfully wielded against the oppressive measures of a corrupt and despotic aristocracy.[25]

The actions of militant unionizers in the 1830s laid the groundwork for working-class actions like the Dorr's Rebellion in Rhode Island in 1843, a suffrage revolt which pitted the interests of the new industrial working class against agrarian based authority.[26] One historian has exclaimed of the revolt that "the rebels gradually and reluctantly came to strive for a measure of popular control over the political process far beyond any yet (or since) achieved in America."[27] Yet it would be after the European revolutions of 1848, which American social observer George Templeton Strong cited as a "democratic influenza," that reformers and planners in New York City, with its burgeoning immigrant population, would earnestly begin devising cultural institutions as a means to control laborers. As New York City historian Anthony Gronowicz recently notes, "The reaction to 1848 . . . [included] efforts at sponsoring temperance and free public schools to compete with taverns and parochial schools not under [American Republican Party] control."[28]

Eric Hobsbawm eloquently describes the "spectre" that haunted American men in power as news came from Europe in 1848:

> [T]he revolution which broke out in the first months of 1848 was not a social revolution merely in the sense that it involved and mobilized all social classes. It was in the literal sense the rising of the laboring poor in the cities . . . of Western and Central Europe. Theirs, and theirs almost alone, was the force that toppled the old regimes from Palermo to the borders of Russia. When the dust settled on their ruins, workers—in France actually socialist workers—were seen to be standing on them, demanding not merely bread and employment, but a new state and society.[29]

Such was the possibility of the scene—"bread or blood"—that confronted Olmsted. The 1848 revolutions were not far from the minds of capitalists after the panic broke in the United States in August of 1857.[30]

The immediate cause of the Panic was the failure of the Ohio Life Insurance and Trust on August 24, but the principal economic cause was overproduction and the overextension of credit. Too much money was in circulation and too little in banks.[31] An 1856 economic report told of unprecedented economic progress: "[T]he year 1856 has given results of which the past has afforded no example. Enormous advance has been made; the cultivation of new territory, the produce of harvests, the extension of factories, the exploitation of mines . . . the railway returns, the spread and improvement of cities."[32] A report on the New York building trades described activity a decade before the panic: "As a whole the period saw . . . the greatest growth that has ever taken place in New York and its contiguous towns. . . . Buildings went up by bounds and blocks; contractors were in ecstasies. . . . The destiny of the metropolis was assured by the adventurous spirit of her business men."[33]

According to a contemporaneous historian, the failure of Ohio Life Insurance and Trust "struck the public mind like a cannon shot. An intense excitement was manifested in all financial circles, in which bank officers participated with unusual sensitiveness and want of self-possession."[34] Bank notes and businesses were rapidly suspended, culminating in the suspension of Wall Street and specie payments on 14 October 1857. As early as September the *New York Times* began a regular column headlined "Hard Times in the City" that reviewed the effect of the crisis on labor, including the labor of building Central Park; on 8 October it read, in part,

> Seven hundred laboring men, who had been employed improving Central Park, were discharged yesterday. . . . The men discharged were mostly Irishmen and Germans, though a few were Italian. The men employed in the manufacture of cabinet work, we are assured by eight heavy dealers . . . will suffer very much from this time forward until spring. Tailors and tailoresses [sweatshop workers], by trade, have a very gloomy prospect before them. . . . All agree that it is not probable that more than one-third of the thousands who are usually thus employed will find work before January next.[35]

Obviously, those hit hardest by the crisis were the working poor, composed, as the *Times* explicitly notes, of recent immigrants, some of whom may have had direct experience in the 1848 revolutions.

Larry J. Reynolds and Sacvan Bercovitch have described the influence of the "revolutionary" threat on mid-century American literature, particularly Hawthorne (although abolitionism and feminist organization, rather than class, are emphasized). As Bercovitch exclaims, the possibility of revolution was sublimated into a literature of containment where dissent was ritually institutionalized and worked more toward national regeneration than social change: "The result was a quasi-dialectic between exclusion and expansion that established, defined, and processually secured the boundaries of the union, a 'new nation' replete with mythic past and 'manifest' future."[36] Analogous to the kind of Hawthornian "quasi-dialectic" that interests Bercovitch is the manufactured Nature of Central Park, which both materially represented a geography of exclusion and rhetorically insisted national expansion, nationhood, and a consensual national identity.

A *Harper's Weekly* article from the midst of the Panic of 1857 explicitly connected Central Park to the suppression of class conflict:

> Our streets have been haunted during the past week by long proces-
> sions of men calling themselves the "Unemployed Workmen," and
> crying aloud for work or bread. . . . The arguments and the oratory are
> familiar in the mouths of the worst demagogues and most mischievous
> disturbers of the public peace in Europe. . . . But are we to let the
> unemployed starve? By no means. Of all the various measures of relief
> which have been proposed, that of proceeding at once with the public
> works [is the most] practical and effective. It is fixed that we are to
> have a new City Hall and a Central Park, the work to be consumed on
> these would more than keep all our unemployed busy all winter.[37]

Threatening dissent, on the revolutionary European model, provides the incentive for Park construction, evidencing an important aspect of the materiality of containment that discloses the ideological agenda that precipitated the enormous capital investments made in the Park.[38]

Inseparable from the economics of market failure were other problems of devaluing that struck New York City, problems all attendant to capital overaccumulation, overproduction, and surplus labor. Urban regions tend toward concentration on a number of planes; that is, the contradiction of the devaluation of the urban center is a profoundly spatial phenomenon. How to resolve this nexus of spatial problems—problems which manifested very real crisis and class violence—was the challenge confronting New York City social planners of the nineteenth century. "[T]he built environment must primarily function to be useful for production, circulation, exchange, and consumption. It is the job of the planner to intervene in the production of this complex composite commodity and to ensure D. Harvey its proper management and maintenance."[39] The built environment must increase the efficiency of the reproduction of the social order; such efficiency was the goal of Olmsted's Central Park project.[40]

This is not to say the Central Park was Olmsted's idea. In fact, politicians and cultural figures began promoting the notion of a large urban park in New York as early as the 1840s. William Cullen Bryant was the first influential advocate; he used the editorial space of his *Evening Post* to announce and to defend the benefits of green space in the city. New York state passed the First Park Act in 1851, an act which was repealed and replaced by the Amended Park Act in 1853. In June 1854, New York City's newly elected democratic mayor, Fernando Wood, authorized a five million dollar expenditure for the greater portion of the land that was to become Central Park. But, with no significant additional investment, the property languished until 1857.

Critics and historians have mistakenly cited partisan politics and a lack of funds as the principal reasons for the relative absence of park development between 1854 and 1857.[41] When the city council finally authorized $250,000 to hire laborers and begin construction in 1857, partisan politics were not neatly resolved and money did not, miraculously, appear. It is more accurate to say that between 1854 and 1857 New York City was not threatened by radical (even revolutionary) spatial devaluation. In 1857 public capital was suddenly and selectively mobilized with a purposive political decision. The "fiscal trigger" of capital mobilization was profound market failure: the Panic of 1857. The urban political scientists Michael A. Pagano and Ann O'M. Bowman explain that "[c]ity officials who perceive market failure within their jurisdictions have choices: either they invest public capital for the purpose of correcting those perceived failures or they allow the marketplace to allocate resources to their most efficient and profitable location."[42] In New York in 1857 market failure was impossible to ignore. Its most obvious effect was high unemployment, low wages, and severe social unrest. Money for Central Park "appeared" in 1857 as a primary intervention intended to control disruption and maintain the value, or arrest the devaluing, of urban space. The most obvious symptom of spatial devaluation was mass unemployment and social conflict; related signs included large departures of recent immigrants, and, ironically, public works projects, like Central Park, that revealed an important kind of municipal/government intervention intended to save the capitalist state from powerful contradictions.

According to the *New York Times* of October 16, 1857, "Every ship for Liverpool now has all the passengers she can carry, and multitudes are applying to work their passage if they have no money to pay for it."[43] News of the reverse tide was a regular feature of the paper. One contributor, signed revealingly, "From the Citizen," expressed xenophobic relief: "One of the effects of the present commercial crisis is an ebb in the hitherto flowing tide of emigration. To see a ship laden with emigrants from America to Ireland is a novel sight. On Saturday last the clipper ship *Dreadnaught* sailed from this port to Liverpool, with three hundred and forty passengers, the largest number ever taken from this country to Europe."[44] The multitude of workers who chose to stay in the United States faced desperate conditions. The regular tabulation of layoffs by the *Times* disclosed the

grim situation that disproportionately affected recent immigrants. Some representatives of the many thousands unemployed took an advertisement in the New York
papers on November 2, which read, "All workmen without employment are hereby
notified to attend a meeting at Tompkins Square. Purpose of meeting—necessity
for prompt, vigorous and decisive action to prevent our families from starving."[45]
In fact, the Tompkins Square "hunger meetings" were precipitated by a refusal on
the part of the New York City Council to act on a public works project suggested
by Mayor Fernando Wood—he asked that money be appropriated for the development of Central Park, a project that would employ thousands.[46] Twelve thousand
unemployed workers attended the Tompkins Square meeting, and on November
5, fifteen thousand attended a similar meeting. These meetings represented a
coalition of unemployed that crossed or ignored ethnic divisions. The papers report
the crowd cheering when one speaker announced that "if one man suffer, it don't
matter whether he is an all American or a foreigner—they all suffer."[47] When no
work was forthcoming some unemployed workers attacked the buildings of flour
merchants and government troops were called out to protect the property of the
capitalists. Finally, *after* the rioting had begun, the City Council set aside
$250,000 for the Central Park project. As Olmsted scholar David Schuyler has
written, "[i]n order to placate the unemployed and provide jobs for as many
workers as possible, in early November the city government allocated enough
money to enable Olmsted to hire one thousand laborers, who worked at clearing
[Central Park] and enclosing it with a wall. Despite innumerable difficulties,
during the first months on the Park Olmsted shaped the one-thousand-man labor
force into 'a capital discipline.'"[48]

Schuyler draws the phrase, "a capital discipline," from Olmsted's own report
on his management of Park workers; the phrase is richly suggestive. Discipline is
the very center of Olmsted's genius and capital the obscured object of his service.
In fact, after the first substantial expenditure on the Park in 1857, the Tompkins
Square protesters moved their demonstration to Central Park, where they spoke
against Mayor Wood's attempt to buy off demonstration leaders with Park jobs and
also against the policy of hiring workers from outside the ranks of demonstrators.[49]
City Hall did acquiesce to some hiring demands, but job tenure was extremely
insecure and the pay low. Men hired to break stone were paid nine cents per cubic
yard. Olmsted exclaimed that "incompetent paupers" had been made to "take 30
or 40 cents a day, that being the exact value of their service in the open market,
instead of a dollar and a quarter a day, which they demanded" (*PFLO* III: 314).
In the interest of discipline and worker turnover (which cycled more workers and
discouraged organized protest), Olmsted ordered that anyone who left "his work
without orders and [did] not return within five minutes, no matter what the cause

of his leaving" would lose his pay for that day, and any worker who left, however shortly, more than twice in half a day was "to be considered as unfit for work and sent away."[50] "Naturally," protest or conflict (let alone any frequency of bodily discharge) was intolerable. Human regulation in the Park took many forms and its importance cannot be overstated. However, the consumption of labor through the employment (and discipline) of potentially violent workers was only one, albeit highly important, aspect of the urban park's significance in terms of maintaining and reproducing social order. It had other, more "invisible" aspects, or, more specifically, the Park was designed as a national, cultural place intended to constitute the consensual identity of ideal citizenship.

Olmsted's construction of Natural space served to obfuscate the productive function of urban, including so-called "natural" space in general. The term "nature," and constructions of Nature, suggest a space outside the network of the built environment. They suggest a space upon which has not yet been built an infrastructure the ultimate form of which is the space of consumption, the safe domestic space. But, in fact, Nature should more accurately be read as the conceptual foundation upon which the space of consumption is built, as it stands as both the subject and object of consumption. It is subject in that it consumes, in the form of financial expenditure and the employment of people, both capital overaccumulation and labor surplus. Thus, by 1866 the Central Park project had employed some 20,000 men and consumed five million dollars.[51] Relatedly, in 1857 and 1858 the American Industrial Association, the New York Association for Improving the Condition of the Poor, and the Woman's Protective Emigrant Society all put forward separate efforts toward the removal of surplus workers to the countryside.[52]

As an object of consumption, "nature" is fetishized into a symbolic condition which easily lends itself to mythological elaboration through a variety of consumable products from land, to landscape art, to popular nature writing. This is the "nature" consumed by the tourist where the experiential expectations are both determined and foreclosed, the landscape inevitably suggesting values like independence and freedom. Gronowicz astutely observes this when he notes in passing that "[d]uller work and longer hours laid emphasis on material enjoyment outside the workplace. . . . Frederick Law Olmsted's Republican park replaced the republican vistas of Jefferson. Visions of homesteads for all workingmen were replaced by a 'central' park where little republicans might mingle with big Republicans and be safely socialized by the latter in a manner that reinforced economic subservience."[53] Nature in the Park is Nature as nation, twisting slightly Jefferson's famous formulation. Which is to say that in "Nature's Nation" the commodification of the central term of identity—"Nature"—was not only foreclosed, but crucially employed as a model of disciplined constitution for the United States' heterogenous population. Nature was a model of harmonious assent, a refining influence, a mirror of stability.

This is particularly obvious according to Olmsted's vision, where Nature was to be consumed as a means of domestication. This was the principal "invisible" function of his Park design, ironically evoking a kind of "spectral" influence to deal with the "spectre" of class conflict. Charles Beveridge, series editor of the Olmsted papers comments that,

> From the [early] time that he became a gentleman farmer, he set himself the task of promoting domesticity . . . he decided that it was the finest and truest expression of civilization. . . . [H]e felt that the chief sign of civilization, as opposed to the barbarism he found on the California frontier, was the desire to have "the enjoyment, the comfort, the tranquility, the morality and the permanent furnishings, interior and exterior, of a home.". . . [H]e asserted that "manifestations of refined domestic life" were "unquestionably the ripest and best fruits of civilization."[54]

Olmsted noted his intention for Boston's Franklin Park, which he called a "Country Park": "To sustain the designed character of the Country Park, the urban elegance generally desired in a small public or private pleasure ground is to be methodologically guarded against. . . . In this respect the park is designed to be an example of throughly nice, though modest and somewhat homespun housekeeping."[55]

To be domesticating Nature should be consumed as landscape. Of course, it had first to be produced as such. Landscapes, as aesthetic idealizations of actual topography, have no clearly definable border and so satisfied the fantasy of infinite space, and, it should also be noted, the psychological illusion of infinite possibility.[56] A space with boundaries fully mapped and perceivable, like the urban space, is closed in terms of both its geographical and psychological topography. Nature becomes the subject of ideological interest and the object of urban reform plans because it functions so well to maintain particular values and illusions, like self-reliance or limitless resources. Thus constructions of Nature at once aggressively strive to control various spaces, with all the bodies they invariably contain, and provide individuals with the rhetoric, either visual, spatial, or verbal, that proves their freedom to themselves. The potential for freedom Nature represents is domesticating to the degree that the suggestion of independence is convincing and knowledge of, or belief that, the condition of dependence, or poverty, or exploitation, which may breed dissatisfaction and unrest, is discouraged; such is one goal of Olmsted's public landscape architecture. However, to understand most fully the function of Central Park as a *cultural* and *constitutional* place, I must here develop the theorization of cultural and aesthetic experience discussed in the introduction by elaborating the history of the philosophy of *culture*.

For the early theorist of culture and aesthetics, Friedrich Schiller, aesthetic culture is the condition of possibility for constituting the political subject. Schiller's theorization of subjectivity occurs in the context of industrialization, urbanization, and social crises (class conflict) of modernity for which Matthew Arnold's later and more famous pronouncements in *Culture and Anarchy* are cognate. In *On the Aesthetic Education of Man*, Schiller writes that, "[a]mong the lower and more numerous classes we are confronted with crude, lawless instincts, unleashed with the loosening of the bonds of civil order, and hastening with ungovernable fury to their animal satisfactions."[57] The fury of the atavistic masses, which must be accounted according to postrevolutionary European anxieties, was the object of Schiller's aesthetic education. Culture was to preserve the burgeoning bourgeois state and attendant capitalist interests from violence and revolution, however these latter were coded in the terms of animalism and barbarism.

To effect the "taming," or civilization, of the threatening masses the modern theory of culture relied on a notion of reformative identification of the individual with the (always idealized) nation. Schiller writes:

> Every individual human being, one may say, carries within him, poten-
> tially and prescriptively, an ideal man, the archetype of a human being,
> and it is his life's task to be, through all his changing manifestations,
> in harmony with the unchanging unity of this ideal. This archetype,
> which is to be discerned more or less clearly in every individual, is
> represented by the State, the objective and, as it were, canonical form
> in which all the diversity of individual subjects strives to unite.[58]

As David Lloyd and Paul Thomas have recently written, culture intervenes between the individual and the state to effect the constitution of the identification that Schiller all but glorifies: "Two conditions make possible this identification: first, that culture . . . represent what it claims to be the fundamentally common identity of all humans; and second, that the state be conceived ideally as the disinterested and ethical representation of this common identity."[59]

Culture constitutes what Arnold termed the "best self" and was the key to the development of such a self. The best self, unlike the ordinary, or finally, for Arnold, the anarchic self, bears and bears upon the unified development of the "whole community," or, as Arnold makes abundantly clear, the state. Class divisions, with their appurtenant parochial interests, restrained the possibility of harmonious disinterest necessary to any legitimate authority governing modern republican society. As Raymond Williams glosses Arnold's idea, "[t]he classes were the embodiment of our ordinary selves: to embody our best self we must create a State."[60] In Arnold's words, "[w]e want an authority, and we find but jealous classes, checks, and a dead-lock; culture suggests the idea of the *State*. We find no basis for a firm State-power in our ordinary selves; culture suggests one to us in our *best self*"[61] (emphasis in original).

Thus culture serves a double, though unified, function: it represents the idea of the ideal state, and it constitutes the individual as an ideal self. Idealism, defined according to terms Arnold provides, is characterized foremost by disinterest and harmony. The ideal, as a condition and guide for political action, engenders politics and culture as conditions of *becoming*. The self and the state are simultaneously *cultivated*, or cultured, through the agency of culture. The organic, or, more precisely, horticultural metaphor is deeply significant and, in some respects, importantly unmetaphorical.

In Central Park Nature is a cultural space. In fact, it is arguably the most promising cultural institution of the era in the United States, according to the meaning and purpose of culture outlined above. The theoretical evidence for this assertion may be found in Schiller, who declared the theater the most promising *theater* aesthetic institution mediating anarchy, individualism, and collective, or, collectively held, authority, or, even more exactly, *representational* authority. As Lloyd and Thomas write, for Schiller, the theater provides "a spatial synthesis that overcomes the contingencies of region and class, to produce an identification of the individual with the figure of universality, 'man.'"[62] Focused on a common object and sharing a single space, the audience is formally collective, and, responding in similar affective ways to theatrical performance, the audience *becomes* similar, proceeds toward an internalized collective identity; they become *universalized,* as Schiller writes: "Effeminate natures are steeled, savages made man, and, as the supreme triumph of nature, men of all ranks, zones, and conditions . . . fraternize here in universal sympathy, forget the world, and come nearer to their heavenly destination. The individual shares in the general ecstacy, and his breast has now only space for one emotion: he is a *man*."[63]

As Schiller makes clear, universality is the necessary condition for political representation; it makes "citizens" of the "masses" by making them representable in a fashion predicated on their being generalizable as "men." Such universalizing engenders paradox and manifold contradictions, not least of which being that the revolution representational politics aimed to contain, by the incorporation of the "masses" with the state, repeatedly disrupts the illusions of representation, most particularly during cycles of economic crisis. I will return to these important complications later, but for now I intend to elaborate and to qualify my assertion above by suggesting that Central Park functioned as a species of Schiller's theatrical space in a tempestuous urban arena and moment.

The problem with theater, which Schiller fails fully to confront, has to do with content, which is tremendously various and difficult to regulate. Various practitioners and theorists, including Artaud and Brecht, came to recognize the manner by which the formal attributes of the theatrical experience hopefully described by Schiller could as well be made to serve a revolutionary agenda. To function effectively for nationalist purposes the spectacle must be regulated. Ideally, the structural position of the spectator would be formally constant and the object of the spectatorial experience would be both uniform and controlled. Lloyd and Thomas, whom I quote at length, have recognized the importance of spatiality and *recreation* to the work of culture as it is articulated in the trajectory from Schiller to Arnold:

> Implicit in the theory of culture is a notion that it is at once recreationary and re-creationary and . . . this pun embodies the deep relation between the *space* of culture and its processes. . . . [T]he efficacy of the aesthetic derives from its pure "determinability," from its not being conditioned by one or the other of the given states or occupations by which humans are divided while at the same time presenting the pure formality of the as-yet-to-be-determined subject with an actual object for its play. In social terms, such a manifestation is only possible in what we have since come to term, for reasons embedded deeply in the very logic of culture's relation to political and economic society, the space of "recreation." That is, only in a space which is set apart from either material or political interests can a object become the undetermined matter for the contemplation of a disinterested subject "at play."[64]

The constitution, or "re-creation," of a universal subject requires a rhetorical and a spatial context of ostensible disinterest. As human beings, in their "ordinary" selves, embody particular interests, the first requirement of culture in disabusing them of interest is its removal from politics. Theater, while formally consistent, has obvious and manifold troubles with the matter of disinterest. Nature, as a strategically constructed experience, brilliantly surmounts the problem of interest. The urban park, and Central Park particularly, was, I reassert, though with added polemic, the penultimate cultural space in nineteenth-century America.

3.

Analyzing the history of landscape representation, the contemporary landscape architect Gina Crandell writes that "there is one great pretense that characterizes landscape architects—we try to disguise the fact that we are actually making boundaries. We do this by calling our designs 'natural.'"[65] Creating manifold boundaries (social and geographic) and generally providing the illusion of limitlessness are principal, if seemingly contradictory, functions of the urban park as Frederick Law Olmsted designed it. Writing to President of the Department of Public Parks H. G. Stebbins in 1872 Olmsted stated that during "fourteen years the whole work of the Central Park centered upon three branches of a single purpose, [the second of which is] the formation of a series of broad, simple meadow surfaces, with, when practicable, such a disposition of umbrageous trees, without underwood, as would render their limits undefined."[66] The following is from "Greensward," Olmsted's winning submission to the contest for the contract to design Central Park: "The horizon lines of the upper park are bold and sweeping and the slopes have great breadth in almost every aspect in which they may be contemplated. As this character is the highest ideal that can be aimed at for a park under any circumstances, and as it is in the most decided contrast to the confined and formal lines of the city, it is desirable to interfere with it, by crossroads and other constructions, as little as possible" (*PFLO* III: 119).

In a section of "Greensward" titled "Motive of the Plan" Olmsted emphasizes the democratic intentions of his "spacious" design:

> The primary purpose of the Park is to provide the best practicable
> means of healthful recreation for the inhabitants of the city, of all
> classes. It should present an aspect of spaciousness and tranquility with
> variety and intricacy of arrangement, thereby affording the most agree-
> able contrast to the confinement, bustle, and monotonous street-divi-
> sion of the city. . . . The Park is intended to furnish healthful recreation
> for the poor and the rich, the young and the old, the vicious and the
> virtuous, so far as each can partake therein without infringing upon the
> rights of others, and no further. (*PFLO* III: 212-13)

Olmsted's segregation of the Park from the city is, according to him, a division of order (tranquility) from disorder (bustle), freedom (spaciousness) from confinement, refinement (intricacy) from monotony. Olmsted contends that the Park itself will be a place of human mixture, but his contention takes the form of a list of binaries and ends with an emphatic announcement of nonmixture, revealing that the geographic segregation of the Park and the city is to be reflected in the separation of human "classes" within the Park. In a nation founded on democratic principles the Park could hardly be sold on the basis of its ability to maintain class differences, but even in the midst of egalitarian rhetoric Olmsted reveals that the Park, as he perceives it, will not threaten (may even elaborate) such differences. Olmsted discloses that the Park (Nature) constitutes social identities by associating natural space with the "virtuous" and "rich" and urban space with the "vicious" and "poor." One is reminded of the "old woman" in Crane's *Maggie*, who takes up her "begging station" at a main entrance to Central Park across from new, and expensive, housing.[67] The wealthy thus have quick access to the Park while the poor wait at the periphery for handouts, the Park itself being a species of handout, however unappreciated. As a founding member of the American Social Science Association Olmsted embraced the Association's charter which emphasized the "responsibilities of the gifted and educated classes toward the weak, the witless, and the ignorant."[68] Olmsted's elitism and conservative reformism were articulated through both his management techniques and his landscape designs, themselves technical marvels intended to manage the conduct of human bodies in space.

It is the lengthy "Greensward" plan of Olmsted and his partner Calvert Vaux that is most often cited as the founding text of landscape design in America. Yet, Olmsted was awarded the job of park superintendent—in charge of labor and police forces—well before the contest to design the Park was opened. He applied for the superintendent position after the panic of 1857 crushed the publishing house (Dix and Edwards) that he had helped to finance and at which he worked (he worked with Thoreau on the *Cape Cod* manuscript and pushed for the publication of Melville's "Benito Cereno"[69]). Heavily in debt and suffering from recurring nervous exhaustion, Olmsted met Charles Elliott—industrialist and member of the newly created New York Commission on Parks—at a Connecticut resort, where Elliott urged his successful application for the position, even though Olmsted had little experience with the scale of management it would require. In fact, he was given the job largely because he was regarded as politically neutral and because he had powerful sponsorship—including endorsements from Washington Irving and William Cullen Bryant.[70] After Olmsted was more or less secure as Park administrator, Vaux (formerly a student of Andrew Jackson Downing, the architect of the Washington Mall) proposed a collaboration with Olmsted on the design for Central Park.[71] In May 1858, after their proposal won over a field of thirty-two, Olmsted was appointed architect in chief for Central Park by the Board of Commissioners, despite an obvious lack of design experience compared to the more qualified Vaux.[72] So, Olmsted became simultaneously chief of discipline (as superintendent) and design. His general lack of qualifications suggest that he was regarded as a political tool, hired to maintain social order and New York's micropolitical order. In fact, Olmsted's two jobs were closely related on the matter of order.

Olmsted gives the impression, in the quote from "Greensward" above, that the landscape offered itself as expansive and that impositions on the geography would corrupt its inherent suggestion of limitlessness, but in fact Olmsted's manipulation of the grounds to achieve such an effect was extraordinary. According to the "Greensward" plan it would be necessary to drain 500 acres at a cost of $30,000; 300,000 trees and shrubs were to be planted ($219,000); half a million dollars was to be spent on building roads and walks (not including over $200,000 for the roads which transverse the Park). As many as 3,600 workers were employed in the construction of the Park at one time.[73] Olmsted himself estimated the quantity of rock and soil moved during construction at nearly five million cubic yards: "or nearly ten-millions of ordinary city one-horse cart-loads, which, in single file, would make a procession thirty thousand . . . miles in length" (*PFLO* III: 43).

The transformation of land into landscape, of space into Nature, the employment of men, and the consumption of capital are the themes of the Central Park's construction. These are the obvious themes, crucial to the Park's mission of defusing class conflict. Protestors turning violent were given shovels and picks and told to move dirt and break rock. The landscape they labored to create was designed to impress the worried or oppressed urban dweller with calming vistas—a spatial rhetoric of leisure that both obscured labor and required it:

> The great advantage which a town finds in a park, lies in the addition
> to the health, strength, and morality which comes from it to its
> people. . . . The reason is obvious: all wealth is the result of labor, and
> every man's individual wealth is, on the whole, increased by the labor
> of every other in the community . . . but as there cannot be the slightest
> exercise of skill of any kind, without the expenditure of force, it fol
> lows that, without recuperation and recreation of force, the power of
> each individual to labor wisely and honestly is soon lost. (*PFLO* VI:
> 106)

Olmsted here proclaims the park's capacity to render the worker physically and morally stronger. Olmsted even subtly suggests that the production of such "wealth" may go to fill the pockets of "workers," though he is too caught up in his idealization to suggest that the wealth may not be evenly distributed. Instead, Olmsted returns to the regulation of the laborer and provides an added inflection to any definition of recreation by attaching it to the concept of force, at once the force of discipline and an economistic metaphor for the agency of capital, which the park is now seen as reproducing. Here, again, is the productive role of the park: it revitalizes the worker and influences him to labor more honestly, by which we may read that it increases his receptivity to his role as an exploited resource. Here *recreation* (re-creation) is most clearly revealed as a meaningful pun.

Geographer David Sibley has recently maintained that space can be either strongly or weakly delimited. Strongly delimited space is characterized by categorization, clear boundaries, nonmixing and, on the part of those invested in the production of such space, paranoia (a hyperbolic fear of contamination). Weakly delimited space is, predictably, characterized by unclear boundaries, mixing and subversion. Sibley himself recognizes that these concepts are themselves categories, representative of the object they have been invented to analyze, yet they can be useful for describing the complex spatial reality of the urban park.[74]

On the one hand Olmsted wanted the urban park sharply differentiated from the surrounding urban environment; all of his plans strove toward "the putting out of view of exterior buildings by a suitable disposition of tall growing trees."[75] On the other hand, he sought, from a perspective within the park, to create a visual and spatial rhetoric of limitlessness. Here was a strongly delimited space in the service of weakly delimited space: the city is quarantined from the park that it may be made seemingly to disappear, while the space of "nature" may appear to recede endlessly. In fact, the urban park can clearly be demonstrated to function as such a weak space according to Sibley's criterion. Thus the need for Olmsted to police the park: its liminal character might attract vagrants and criminals, the socially outcast who prey on the "honest" worker and middle-class stroller. The urban park, from its use by the queer to its staging of the carnivalesque and the acts of the criminal is, we have come to know, rife with subversion. But here, also, such subversion is expected, open to inspection, and contained. The park is far less a strongly delimited space in the service of limitlessness (though this it is), than an apparently weakly delimited space in the service of law, order, stability, and profit.

For Olmsted Central Park was not a space for physical engagement either with "nature" or in sporting competitions with other people, but an object of contemplation according to aesthetic principles. Olmsted came into conflict with city commissioners over the matter of policing the Park because, rather than identify and control typical crimes, Olmsted wanted Park police to manage how people interacted with the space—he wanted to protect the Park from the "shock of an untrained public."[76] As an aesthetic object the Park offered "training" in disinterest, or, an "abstraction of the [individual] from his embeddedness in particularity."[77] This is, precisely, the "cultivation" of the individual through a "natural" institution whereby he or she is spatially and rhetorically inserted into a narrative that suggests a "harmonious" development of human potential to match the grand harmony of the nation for which the Park stands. Nature unfolds before the individual, calmly insisting a material and metaphoric model of social and individual harmonious objectives. Nature, or the Park as a cultural institution under the guise of "nature," becomes a formative principle of the capitalist states' efficacy in repressing conflict by offering an ideal developmental narrative. The terms of conflict—social differences of condition, the individual versus the capitalist state, particularist interests versus the universalist nation—are occluded by the confusion inimical to a "weak" space thoroughly and strategically designed.

Olmsted's biographer, Laura Wood Roper, writes the following of the urban context at the time Central Park construction was initiated: "[W]hen [Olmsted] took charge of the largest public work in New York, public order there was in dark eclipse. It had been declining all through the 1840s, when a million and a half European immigrants had poured into the city, many of them to crowd and stagnate its sordid and degrading slums. There gangs, native and foreign born, fought and slaughtered each other; in better neighborhoods footpads, pickpockets, prostitutes, and beggars operated busily."[78] If Central Park was intended to clean up the streets it would not only need to remove from them a great number of unemployed, which it did, but also act, according to Olmsted (or, in fact, Roper, whose picture, as I will show, may be inaccurate), as an agent of social hygiene in a perceived situation of physical and moral pollution: it would have to coerce a "rowdy" population to honest and clean living. Olmsted and the commissioners who initiated the Central Park project certainly recognized that the space of Nature they planned was likely to be the site of transgressive activity, but it was precisely in an effort to control perceived transgression that it was constructed. Such an ambiguous space, neither urban nor rural, both "natural" and man made, was necessarily conducive to the transgression it was designed to control. The advantage of the Park was that, viewed from the outside, from the tall buildings and offices that have come to surround it, it lay as a severely delimited space, policeable both at its borders, and, as Olmsted was first hired to assure, in its interior. As Olmsted wrote in his application for the superintendent position, "I have visited and examined as a student most of the large parks of Europe . . . and while thus engaged have given special attention to *police details* and the employment of labor in them" (*PFLO* III: 76, my emphasis).

The first charge of the Park police was the removal of the people who lived in the space the Park was to be built. The *New York Times* reported on the obstacle they represented in July of 1856:

> West of the reservoir, within the limits of the Central Park, lies a neat

little settlement, known as "Nigger Village." The Ebon inhabitants,
after whom the village is called, present a pleasing contrast in their
habits and the appearance of their dwellings to the Celtic occupants, in
common with hogs and goats, of the shanties in the lower part of the
Park. They have been notified to remove by the first of August. The
policemen find it difficult to persuade them out of the idea which has
possessed their simple minds, that the sole object of the authorities in
making the Park is to procure their expulsion from the homes which
they occupy.[79]

Several points may be derived from this rich passage. There is the media attempt
to diminish the actual presence of many people (5,000 by some estimates) by
emphasizing a "little settlement" and by using the pejorative "Nigger Village" for
the actual name, Seneca Village—erasing presence and voice through hegemonic
nomination. Also, a general equation is drawn of Irish, blacks, hogs, and
goats—the common epistemological lowering strategy of racism. Finally, the
passage demeans the inhabitants' intelligence precisely as it discloses their deep
insight, for a principal function of the Park was their removal. As one newspaper
reported, "If the opening of the park raises the actual or speculative value of lands
in its vicinity, it is certain that the poorer class of citizens will not settle them
extensively when homesteads can be obtained cheaper elsewhere."[80]

The dominant image of the settlements in the upper island area of Central
Park was one of filth, transience, and criminality. The Park's first engineer
described people "dwelling in rude huts of their own construction, and living off
the refuse of the city. . . . These people who had thus overrun and occupied the
territory were principally of foreign birth, with but very little knowledge of the
English language, and with very little respect for the law."[81] A report in the *Times*
on March 5, 1856 describes it as an area of "human misery, poverty, and degradation . . . inhabited principally by Irish families, who dwell in specimens of architecture so rickety . . . that they might make one tremble with apprehension for
their inmates."[82]

As Roy Rozenzweig and Elizabeth Blackmar have presented in their history
of the Park, such images were an invention. The stability of the population was
remarkably greater than in most urban regions: "Virtually every black family in
Seneca Village recorded by the 1850 census was still there five years later. . . . 40
percent of Boston's population moved in those same five years" and blacks had
generally higher mobility rates than others in most urban areas.[83] The term "shan-
ty," used so often in discussions of the communities, was meant to evoke poverty
and transience, yet the surviving records show that, like most other Irish and
blacks in New York, those who settled in the Park worked in service labor and

were not destitute. Though they could never be called wealthy, the inhabitants of Seneca Village possessed landholdings above those of comparable ethnic enclaves in any other part of the city: "With more than half the black households in Seneca Village in 1855 owning property, African-Americans there had a rate of property ownership five times as great as New Yorkers as a whole" and thirty-nine times greater than other blacks in the city.[84] Rozenzweig and Blackmar conclude that "ironically, a settlement that contemporary and historical accounts depict as disorganized and degraded may have been one of the pillars of New York's antebellum black community."[85]

In Seneca Village the ideological manner by which race obscures class is obvious. The Park discussions in the newspapers and the descriptions by those involved in Park construction, rhetorically "construct" the people as vagrants and criminals—in the fact of its building many of them may have become such—but historical research reveals a stable and more-or-less prosperous community. Race, as an "outward sign," becomes the shade through which class is viewed, effectively rendering the two categories synonymous. The stable community is imperceptible while race, as an essentialist or biological category, comes to stabilize class difference. Prosperity and community become the attributes of whiteness in this negative manner, where blackness or Irishness are only perceived according to images of poverty, including filth and transience. If exceptionalism functions to obscure class difference, then here we see how race functions in an exceptionalist manner by rendering class difference as racial difference. The black or immigrant is essentially condemned to lower-class status while at the same time class as a social category becomes imperceptible and race obvious. Class difference is reinforced by racial invention.

In 1856, with the arrival of the Park police, previously accepted activity within the Park became criminalized. Cutting trees for firewood, an unenforced municipal statute, became a zealously punished offense. Likewise, the previously common self-employment of breaking stones and selling them as pavement was criminalized. Finally, under such pressures, the Park residents left their homes without incident on October 1, 1857.[86] The papers, filled with news of the Panic, did not report their departure.[87] Two weeks later the contest to design the ground was opened. A heterogenous space had been cleared of inhabitants, leaving a rough and muddy scene awaiting a design that could "universalize" the interests of increasingly conflicted classes.

By Olmsted's intention the control of social behavior and the elaboration of social difference was Nature's finest function. I would venture, agreeing with Crandell above, that all of Olmsted's landscape engineering is an effort of social control where the work of the engineer is intended to be impossible to detect. As

Olmsted wrote of his landscape design for the World's Columbian Exposition in Chicago, "the thing is to make it appear that you found this body of water and its shores and have done nothing to them except at the landing and bridges. They were rich, rank, luxurious, crowded with vegetation, like the banks of some tropical rivers that I have seen on Louisiana bayous. The vegetation must appear spontaneous and thoroughly wild (to all unlearned visitors)."[88] Olmsted repeatedly asserted that a primary purpose of his park designs was to provide "civilizing" benefits for the urban poor, or, as he writes in the above quote, the "unlearned." He proposed an invisible but rigorous influence: "A park is a work of art, designed to produce certain effects upon the mind of men. There should be nothing in it, absolutely nothing—not a foot of surface nor a spear of grass—which does not represent study, design, a sagacious consideration and application of known laws of cause and effect with reference to that end."[89]

The urban poor, according to Olmsted, were threatened by "an anxious and narrowly dogged habit of mind and a strong incitement to persistent toilsome industry."[90] The urban park was deployed to restrain their incitement: "Do your duty to them or they will not do their duty to you."[91] Nature, as he imagined and designed it, was to offer "a distinctly harmonizing and refining influence upon the most unfortunate and most lawless classes of the city,—an influence favorable to courtesy, self-control, and temperance."[92]

As Horace Greeley makes clear, the park was imagined as a space that erased social distinctions; in arguing for a public park he asserted that "the aesthetic faculties need to be educated—drawn out . . . there need to be places and times for re-unions [so that] the rich and poor, the cultivated and the well-bred and the sturdy and self-made shall be attracted together and encouraged to assimilate."[93] Greeley immediately, if unintentionally, discloses that he will bear no threat to his identity; only the very vague term "poor" can likely be attached to anyone not like himself. In effect he is saying that those who already represent the hegemonic national/class ideal need a park to be reassured of their hegemony, to reinforce the constituency of national control.[94] However, Olmsted disguised this self-reflecting function in a language of assimilation. Writing about his design for the new state agricultural colleges, intended to educate (in practical matters) those outside educational class privileges, he explains that he seeks to create social homogeneity. It was very important, he felt, that "everyone reads similar books, wears similar clothing, has similar arguments, and dwells in a similar house with similar furniture" (PFLO VI: 276). It is a safe assertion that this was, for him, a social and architectural goal beyond the community of the new "experimental" colleges and that it informed his decisions with regard to Central Park. The actual process of building a place like Central Park was both disruptive (evicting stable communities) and stabilizing (helping to relieve the anxieties of the more-or-less privileged), but it did nothing to make threatening social differences disappear, other than from view.

The threat of difference (and conflict)—difference that is, for capitalism, both necessary and necessary to obscure—worried the professional classes most interested in the Park. The genius of the deployment of the Park—and the measure of effectiveness for cultural institutions—was in universalizing interests while maintaining differences: in short, the genius of American exceptionalism. According to Olmsted it was the "cultivated classes" who "stood in the vanguard of our civilization, they are our stronghold against agrarian and nihilistic tendencies. They are the best security we have in our immanent perils of personal and mercenary politics."[95] Thus, in his suburban design projects, he sought to protect class composition by imposing minimal limits on the cost of homes and specific design features for the homes.[96] In seeming contradiction to his frequently articulated desire for a gathering place for all classes in his urban parks, Olmsted proposed with his suburban designs that homes be set back forty feet from the road and at least ten feet from the sides of the lot (*PFLO* V: 278).[97] The suburban home was intended to be a severely protected middle-class space, strongly delimited according to Sibley's terms, made for an expanding professional class anxious, precisely, about their class security. This deep anxiety could be relieved by spatially constituting distinctions that were, in urban space, anything but clear, as such space was characterized by ambiguity and heterogeneity. Early records of Central Park usage, like those of landscape philosophy already reviewed, suggest a similar purpose.

The *New York Herald* announced the Park as "the great rendezvous of the polite world."[98] The majority of Park users came in carriage or horseback (relatively expensive means of transportation) and participated, willingly or not, in promenades of social competition and distinction (recall the epigraph from Whitman). Of those who came on foot, Rozenzweig and Blackmar report, "few came from the city's poorest neighborhoods."[99] On this matter Olmsted's police have left excellent surveillance records: "The gatekeepers recorded the daily rhythm of Park use in meticulous attendance logs. In the mid-1860s, about half the visitors entered between 3 and 6 P.M.; 4 to 5 P.M. was the most popular carriage-driving hour." Rozenzweig and Blackmar comment on the pattern: "New Yorkers whose carriage ritual most commonly peaked between 4 and 5 P.M. but shifted with the seasons had a great deal of control over their leisure time. They were older retired men; middle-aged men wealthy enough to have retired early or powerful enough to set their own hours; young men enjoying their family's affluence; and . . . women of what Thorstein Veblen would soon call 'the leisure class.'"[100] Olmsted's Park was productive of, and a showcase for, distinction(s).

The anthropologist Edmund Leach describes the contradictions of strong spatial distinctions: "The more sharply we define our boundaries, the more conscious we become of the filth that has ambiguously got onto the wrong side of the frontier. Boundaries become dirty by definition and we devote a great deal of effort to keeping them clean, just so that we can preserve confidence in our category system."[101] Sibley concisely states a historic fact when he writes that the "poor as a source of pollution and moral danger were clearly identified in contemporary accounts of the nineteenth-century capitalist city."[102] Class difference became expressed, and repressed, in terms of geography: the rich took to the airy "height," Olmstedian suburb, or Park, where they sought to protect themselves from the lowly poor and their diseases. On the one hand, the urban park was described by Olmsted as a kind of border region where the "polluted" and the pure (to use Leach's terms) were to mix company, thus, through sheer contact and the "invisible" influence of Nature, refining the poor, re-creating them through "recreation." On the other hand, while designed to combat the manifold representatives of disease and disorder, it served to heighten to a fever pitch the paranoia of infection. The pure green space of the park, metaphor of the health of the nation and the individual, could not, finally, be kept clean. Today we know that such disruptive reminders of economic violence as the homeless have never been absent from Central Park (around five thousand people were originally evicted); in fact, they have become more obvious. The ineradicable presence of such poverty may have spawned reform efforts (like park building), but not progress, as the deep contradictions that the Park both manifests and represents subsume reform as part of an undisclosed charter that pretends to erase poverty while playing a crucial role in preserving an economic system infinitely productive of violent exploitation.

For instance, before the first tenement law was passed in 1857 lawmakers were fundamentally unwilling to infringe the liberal rights of usage for private property.[103] The Panic of 1857, and the ensuing class conflicts, frightened them enough that they listened to the pleas not necessarily of the poor themselves, but of the reformers who identified environment as the prime cause of moral and physical delinquency: "From the 1830s commentators had readily blamed riots, disease, crime and immorality on housing conditions; and with the depression of the 1840s, the Astor Place riot and cholera epidemic of 1849, the citywide strike wave in 1850, and the police riot and demonstrations by the unemployed in 1857, editors and reformers asserted the connection between civil disorder, epidemics, and housing conditions with increased vigor."[104]

Of course, as reformers dutifully (as exceptionalist functionaries) reported, many tenement houses were simply uninhabitable, and yet the tenants were often under contractual obligation to pay rents to absent landlords. A general shortage of housing left them little choice anyway. Urban reformers sought to eliminate vast tracts of tenement housing and in place construct parks, boulevards, and quality apartments. Unfortunately, "analysis of lower-class neighborhoods allowed upper-class reformers to speak for the poor with consummate authority. Municipal efforts were unleashed without any corresponding increase in lower-class power to influence policies."[105] Public works reform projects displaced thousands with no attempts to secure alternative shelter. The reformer and sensationalist Jacob Riis considered the actions in Mulberry Bend as "the great triumph in his 'ten years' war' against the slum."[106] The area was cleared under the Small Parks Act legislation: the tenements of the poor were crushed to make room for Columbus Park. The poor who left the area moved to nearby tenements, many of which were also soon cleared to make way for living quarters too expensive for the workers to afford. Riis himself estimated that the project displaced 10,000 people.[107] He might also have considered how dramatically the value of urban space around the Park had increased.

Reformers, often in collusion with real estate developers, pushed for greater property condemnation and excavation, arguing that the efforts "could recoup the cost of public improvements and renew neighborhoods when cities auctioned the abutting strips to private developers. . . . They claimed that excess condemnation had been working quiet miracles since the 1880s, when enhanced property assessments accompanied the completion of Central Park."[108] Olmsted's Central Park had set a precedent for increasing the value of urban space, though this was effected, or certainly intended effects, along more and other fronts than that of exchange value.

During the Panic of 1857, the city government ordered that Olmsted discharge seven hundred Central Park workers, only to hire a larger number of workers the next week. It was between the firing and the hiring that the episode—"bread or blood"—occurred. As I have already suggested, Olmsted's jobs as director of labor and police were in fact identical, as workers one day were protesters the next—a result of the city's effort to appease as many as possible over the short term. Thus, workers crowded into urban space and without adequate resources for themselves or their families were protesting their treatment as they were constructing a landscape intended to convince them of the endless resources at their disposal and constitute them according to the "universal" terms of culture. *This, here, after A's above is more to the point*

The massive effort and expense that went into building Central Park testifies to an overaccumulation of capital, but the very fact of the Park's size, not to mention its vistas, insists a fantasy of overabundant space. If there was not enough space available for all to enjoy the plentitude of America, so the ideological vision the Park insists runs, then certainly what was available would not be wasted on the luxury of an urban park. The Park was constructed in keeping with the idealized landscape of an unlimited America, the prime symbology of which could be located in the West. It was in the "frontier" that Olmsted would begin to theorize, and also to materialize, in a form of hysteria, the insistence of distinctions amid and seemingly in contradiction to the universalizing effects of culture at the center of his landscape designs, social philosophy, and personal sense of self. He would also help to realize, again, the "value" of Nature for capital through his variously aesthetic, political, and economic promotion, management, and design of "natural" (and both actually and ostensibly unproductive) space.

Chapter Two

Olmsted's Failure: Yosemite, Culture, and Productivity

> I have been in the habit of watching men at work, and of judging of their industry, their skill, their spirit; in short, of whatever goes to make up their value to their employers, or to the community, as instruments of production.
>
> —Olmsted in *The Cotton Kingdom: A Traveller's Observations on Cotton and Slavery in the American Slave States, 1853-1861*

> I am very well, so long as I don't think. . . . Prey keep on thinking of me for what I was (as unfortunate women say).
>
> —Olmsted to F. N. Knapp, 28 September 1864

I opened the previous chapter asserting Whitman's unconcern for "disguising" the erotic content of his experiences was related to his insights about Central Park's privileged patrons—how their grooming was reflected by the "groomed" Nature of the Park. Whitman's exchange with the Park officer at once revealed his preference for unmediated "nature," and revealed the Park's service in disguising social relations, its removal of "roughs" and enforced constitution of a harmoniousness for which Nature stood as a prime symbol and model. Likewise, there is an erotic content in the Olmsted quotations above. The first enunciates the classic cross-racial desire described so brilliantly by Leslie Fiedler in *Love and Death and the American Novel*: Huck comes to Jim, Ishmael to Queequeg, Natty to Chinchinga-gook, in a pattern that represents the futile desire—for which homoerotic desire works as a substitute—to preserve or regain an individual and national innocence, a trope which is itself a kind of ideological clouding of the social conditions and

[handwritten margin notes:] actually he opens w/ the parade of possessions — besides it's a park + policeman who is the object of? This erotic movement no word of that? there is? Chinga-Chgook ?

41

patterns of modernity in the United States. Olmsted, as a voyeur of the slave at work, wrests this trope from literary tradition and places it firmly in the blooming discourse of sociological reformism. Though Olmsted, whose self-discipline was obsessive, is unable to acknowledge the erotic content of his observations, he explicitly articulates the concern with production that characterized the arguments of slavery's apologists *and* detractors.

I will develop the precise terms of Olmsted's views on both slavery and production in this chapter, but before proceeding I wish to admit the personal inflection of Olmsted's professional engagements that is evident in my second epigraph. This remark—composed while working as a manager for the Mariposa Gold Mine in California—emerged as Olmsted confronted what he registered as the last in a series of professional failures. A constant and uncompromising spokesperson for refinement and civility, failure, according to Olmsted above, rendered him a whore. He considered himself used, his dignity evaporated. Olmsted experienced a profound and painful emotional crisis while in Mariposa; the quote above is as close as he came to identifying the crisis as a kind of ontological falling. Placed alongside his own theorization of the conditions of barbarism and civilization, these latter, Olmsted's "social" concerns, are revealed as a deep, and disappointing, self-examination. In short, in a barely conscious fashion Olmsted came to describe the terms of his own confused condition. Enormously invested in the promotion of civilization, Olmsted elaborated a social schematic, or a kind of taxonomy, where he was the savage.

Olmsted was a representative member of a socially engaged, growing, mobile, and, I would emphasize, anxious professional class.[1] Olmsted's confusion of the social and the personal reveals this anxiety. The central contention of this chapter is that Olmsted's decisive involvement with the creation of Yosemite Park during his tenure in California represents another exceptionalist deployment of Nature, one which particularly reveals the abjection, even hysteria, of the class, and class interests, Olmsted represented. Other themes, which develop those introduced previously, involve the role of Yosemite in the dialectic of value and devalue. Further, I advance my analysis of culture as a deployed space by examining in greater detail Olmsted's writings and the complex form of his thoughts on the subject of political progress and the cognate categories of "barbarism" and "civilization." Olmsted's serious engagement with these subjects began with his investigations, as a correspondent for the *New York Times*, into the economic situation of slavery and the South.

1. Slave State Travels and Reform

Olmsted resigned from his various duties with Central Park shortly after the start of the Civil War.[2] A staunch and verbally aggressive social reformist (though, as I explain below, by no standard an abolitionist), Olmsted possessed an extraordinary sense of mission for the Union cause, and though physically unable to serve as a soldier in the conflict—he suffered permanent injury from a carriage accident—he was not to be left out from some important service. At the start of the War Olmsted hoped to be appointed to superintend "contraband," or slaves taken by the Union. Olmsted wrote to his friend Henry Bellows: "I have, I suppose, given more thought to the special question of the proper management of negroes in a state of limbo between slavery & freedom than any one else in the country. I think, in fact, that I should find here my 'mission,' which is really something I am pining to find in this war."[3] Olmsted hoped to affect slaves as he hoped Central Park affected the urban poor.

By 1861 Olmsted was already established as a respected critic of slavery, having authored several volumes on the South which highlighted the social and economic conditions, and perceived consequences, of the institution.[4] Yet, Olmsted was not an abolitionist, radical, reformist, or otherwise. In the introduction to the most recent edition of Olmsted's *The Cotton Kingdom*, Arthur M. Schlesinger correctly summarizes that "Olmsted's own solution [to slavery] was gradual manumission by the action of the slaveholders themselves."[5] Olmsted strategized negotiating with Southerners before his travels, explaining that the best way was to "*reason* with them as though *we might* be the mistaken ones, for truly I think in my heart we *may* be."[6] The possible Northern mistake *was* abolitionism, which Olmsted regarded as a profound and threatening violation of his notions of culture and the progress of civilization.

Critics often find Olmsted's attitude toward slavery and the South confused by such declarations as the following, from his introduction to *The Cotton Kingdom*: "It is said that the South can never be subjugated. It must be, or we must. It must be, or not only our American republic is a failure, but our English justice and our English law and our English freedom are failures."[7] As his prompt slip from things American to things English reveals, Olmsted's concern with slavery is subsumed by his concern with "civilization." Olmsted was not troubled to criticize slavery on moral grounds, but according to economic principles, his developing ideas of nationalism and, relatedly, progress:

> Subjugation! I do not choose the word, but take it, and use it in the only
> sense in which it can be applicable. This is a Republic, and the South
> must come under the yoke of freedom, not to work for us, but to work

with us, on equal terms, as a free people. To work with us, for the security of a state of society, the ruling purpose and tendency of which, spite all of its bendings heretofore, to the necessities of slavery; spite all of the incongruous foreign elements which it has had constantly to absorb and incorporate . . . has, beyond all question, been favorable to sound and safe progress in knowledge, civilization, and Christianity.[8]

For Olmsted, slavery was not categorically wrong ("the yoke of freedom"?); he wrote exactly as much in the *New York Times* in 1854: "I do not consider slaveholding . . . in itself, necessarily wrong, any more than all forcible constraint of a child or lunatic is wrong."[9] Earlier, in March of 1853, Olmsted wrote declaratively that "The Negroes are a degraded people, degraded not merely by position, but actually immoral, low-lived; without healthy ambition, but little influenced by high moral considerations, and in regard to labor not . . . affected by regard for duty."[10] Despite these limited views, Olmsted did regard slavery a corruption in need of reformation, but besides what Olmsted perceived as its inhibition of economic progress was slavery's negative relation to culture.

   Olmsted's understanding of slavery's relation to culture is suggested by the fact that *Cotton Kingdom* is dedicated to John Stuart Mill, to whose political philosophy of progressive republicanism Olmsted was strongly attached. Slavery, for Olmsted, may have promoted the prosperity of classical Greek culture, but it had emphatically the opposite effect in the United States, which was precisely its threat to political progress. Olmsted's writings on the South were offensive, and likely still are, to Southerners. They offer a veritable encyclopedia, with rare exception, of Southern ineptitude. Olmsted, in fact, spends less time in *Cotton Kingdom* discussing slaves than he does whites, both of whom he implicates as unfit for the responsibilities of citizenship. Regarding Southern whites, he inveighs the absence of Christian values, clergymen, and congregations and explains that the "reason for this is the same with that which explains the general ignorance of the people of the South: the effect of slavery in preventing social association of the whites, and in encouraging vagabond and improvident habits of life among the poor."[11] In a letter to Charles Loring Brace, Olmsted despairs of having something new or interesting to say about the slaveholders he meets in the lower South: "[T]here's nothing to be said that can't be put into one letter. They are all the same—just . . . half-brutes, half-gentlemen" (*PFLO* II: 210).

   Olmsted's stated objective for his Southern travels was the determination of slavery's various effects developed and understood through a disinterested appraisal of the economics of slavery. White Southerners, as Olmsted saw, held the laborer in contempt and, as a consequence, the value of labor was itself degraded. Slaves, with no motivation other than punishment, labored inefficiently, and were, according to Olmsted, tremendously overvalued by the standards of the free labor market. Thus, Southerners, even the more-or-less wealthy, carried high debt and lacked the capital for civil or domestic improvement. The combination of fiscally overvalued laborers and socially undervalued labor devastated the South's opportunities for moral, economic, and, relatedly, domestic progress. Olmsted's concern with domesticity as a gauge of civilization is emphasized by the extensively detailed descriptions of the homes he passes or at which he stays. The following is a summary description of the dwellings of the typical, or most numerous, slaveholders:

> The large majority of the dwellings were of logs. . . . The logs are usually hewn but little; and, of course, as they are laid up, there will be wide interstices between them—which are increased by subsequent shrinking. These, very commonly, are not "chinked," or filled up in any way; nor is the wall lined on the inside. Through the chinks, as you pass along the road, you may often see all that is going on in the house; and, at night, the light of the fire shines brightly out on all sides.[12]

Olmsted met little of the grand wealth and elevated manners that Northerners commonly thought characterized the South. With only infrequent exception, he met degradation and "barbarity." Yet, despite his acute understanding that slavery was the prime cause of the South's evils, he would not, as we have seen, condone abolition. The Union, as he envisioned it as harmonious and civilized, could not bear the charge, let alone the influence, of such a mass of barbarians, white and black. Olmsted read J. S. Mill seriously, and fully agreed with Mill's pronouncements in *Considerations on Representative Government*:

> [A] people in a state of savage independence, in which every one lives for himself, exempt, unless by fits, from any external control, is practically incapable of making any sort of progress in civilization unless it has learnt to obey. The indispensable virtue, therefore, in a government which establishes itself over a people of this sort is, that it make itself obeyed. . . . [U]ncivilized races . . . are averse to continuous labor of an unexciting kind. Yet all real civilization is at this price; without such labor, neither can the mind be disciplined into the habits required by civilized society, nor the material world be prepared to receive it.[13]

At the center of Mill's theory of political progress is discipline; he accepts slavery and despotism as unfortunate but often necessary stages in the progress of civilization and his political ideal: representative government. But this rule of the savage—or, as Mill explicitly states, the worker—by force is gradually supplemented by enlightened guidance or contact with "cultured" spheres of civilized political behavior: "It is by political discussion that the manual laborer, whose employment is a routine, and whose way of life brings him in contact with no variety of impressions, circumstances and ideas . . . whose daily occupations concentrate his interests in a small circle round himself, learns to feel for and with his fellow citizens, and becomes consciously a member of a great community."[14] As Raymond Williams has demonstrated, Mill drew his faith in and idea of culture from Coleridge, especially his volume, the *Constitution of Church and State*, where Coleridge writes:

> The permanency of the nation . . . and its progressiveness . . . depend on a continuing and progressive civilization. But civilization is itself but a mixed good, if not far more a corrupting influence, the hectic of disease, not the bloom of health, and a nation so distinguished more fitly to be called a varnished than a polished people, where this civilization is not grounded in cultivation, in the harmonious development of those qualities and faculties that characterize our humanity.[15]

Mill and Coleridge provide the particular philosophical background of Olmsted's political and cultural views on the South. In all of his endeavors Olmsted acted as if the fate of civilization, the nation, and the very possibility of political progress were at stake. The concept of cultivation, which suggests culture's relation to organic notions of controlled development, pointedly locates Olmsted's reformist practices (landscape architecture and labor management) and beliefs. In fact, Olmsted's use of the term implies pedagogical prescription, as when he writes of the need with regard to slaves for "cultivating habits which are necessary to be cultivated, before the manliest child of white men is capable of enjoying freedom."[16] Accordingly, cultivation is inseparable from paternalism. Thus, during his Southern travels in 1853, Olmsted writes to Brace on the matter of Northern "barbarism" among the working classes: "We need institutions that shall more directly *assist* the poor and degraded to elevate themselves. Our educational principles must be enlarged and made to include more than these miserable common schools. The poor & wicked need more than to be let alone" (*PFLO* II: 234). Those deemed unfit for full participation in republican governance must be carefully tended and taught—by the agents and agency of culture—proper beliefs and behavior, or, in short, the disciplined terms of citizenship. Olmsted concludes his letter by instructing Brace to "go ahead with the Children's Aid [Society] and get up *parks*, gardens, music, dancing schools, reunions which will be so attractive as to force into contact the good & the bad, the gentlemanly and the rowdy" (*PFLO* II: 236, my emphasis).

It bears mentioning—in the interest of clarifying Olmsted's beliefs—that his enthusiastic response to the Continental revolutions of 1848 does not contradict his paternalism.[17] In this case Olmsted again reveals the influence of Mill and the liberal philosophy intended to mediate rapid political transformations by his regard for aristocratic systems as "relics of barbarism."[18] Popular European revolutions were also republican revolutions; as a moderate Olmsted fails to celebrate the specifically socialist aspects of these antiaristocratic revolts.

In simplest terms the South and the majority of its constituents, both black and white, stood, according to Olmsted, as an obstacle to political, which is to say national, progress. His preferred term for national ideals and goals was "civilization." His preferred agent for effecting civilization was *culture* and the process was *cultivation*.[19] His development of "natural" spaces must be understood according to the meaning he gave these critical terms. Olmsted's activities in the West as labor manager and as a promoter and later commissioner of Yosemite Park must likewise be analyzed and evaluated according to his understanding of these terms.

2. Mariposa and Yosemite

The violent dynamics of spatial production discussed in chapter one are reiterated in the Mariposa/Yosemite region in a form similar to that described for Central Park and in a form inflected with the characteristics of imperialist, frontier spatial production. Henri Lefebvre, in his model of the imperialist transformation of "absolute" (outside the network of capitalism) to "abstract" (incorporated) space, shrewdly pronounces the affiliation of culture and violence. His emphasis is drawn in the context of the imperialist state's confrontation with "absolute" sovereignty:

> Sovereignty implies "space," and what is more it implies a space against which violence . . . is directed. . . . Only by violence could technical, demographic, economic and social possibilities be realized. . . . [E]very state is born of violence, and state power endures only by virtue of violence directed towards a space . . . imposing laws upon it and carving it up administratively according to criteria quite alien to the initial characteristics of either the land or its inhabitants. . . . A founding violence, and continuous creation by violent means—such are the hallmarks of the state. But the violence of the state must not be viewed in isolation: it cannot be separated either from the accumulation of capital or from the rational and political principle of *unification*, which subordinates and totalizes the various aspects of social prac-

tice—legislation, culture, knowledge, education—within a determinate
space; namely, the space of the ruling class's hegemony over its people
and over the nationhood that it has arrogated.[20]

The Yosemite region was the sovereign space of the Miwok Indians before it
was violently appropriated as the nationalist and, as Olmsted would make clear, the
cultural space of a re-creative park. Olmsted employed culture as a tool to transform or produce spaces of manifold contestations—on the terms of labor dispute
at the Mariposa Estate and Native/national sovereignty in Yosemite—into places
intended to advance his qualified national republicanism. Ideally, for Olmsted, the
areas he managed would function as spaces of national and nationalist identity
formation, though the emotional crisis he experienced while in the West would
reveal crucial contradictions inherent in such hegemonic cultural articulations.

Interpreting the complex contributing factors responsible for Yosemite Park's
justification and establishment through Olmsted's involvement reveals social and
political dynamics that Yosemite Park critics and historians have neglected to
develop. Alfred Runte, the most influential Yosemite Park historian, rightly notes
that tourists promoted the idea that "Yosemite, symbolically, might mean their
culture," even as he mistakenly equates such popular promotions with the actual
opinion of most Americans.[21] Runte's confusion on this account bears association
with the general promotional tone of his volume. Thus he cites the fact that an
agent for transportation interests set the Park idea in motion but fails to develop its
implications. Instead, Runte simply reiterates the rhetorical justification of financially interested parties by asserting the "preservation principles" to which Park
legislators held firm. Runte is caught up in the very exceptionalist mode the Park
itself elaborates when he neglects to explore the paradox of capitalists interested
in the promotion of *public* property.[22]

Two recent considerations of Yosemite, one by the cultural critic Rebecca
Solnit and the other by historian Mark Spence, have begun to describe the history
and dynamics of Yosemite's violent incorporation into the national and nationalist
network. Spence's work focuses on what he terms the "national park ideal" and its
relation to Native "dispossession." His thorough study explores the history of
Native presence in the Yosemite region and the struggle, through a good part of the
twentieth century, of Yosemite Indians to maintain viable communities in the Park.
Remarking on the cultural elaboration of the "wilderness ideal," Spence writes that
what, for instance, "[Ansel] Adams's photographs [of Yosemite] obscure, and what
tourists, government officials and environmentalists fail to remember, is that the
uninhabited wilderness had to be created. . . . At base, the wilderness preserved in
national parks, monuments, and forests is a wilderness dispossessed—dispossessed
of the people who shaped and were shaped by their interaction with it over the

course of centuries."[23]

Rebecca Solnit is likewise concerned with recording the historical process of dispossession. Solnit emphasizes the violence of Native removal and, in an intriguing and often moving fashion, relates Native removal to what she calls "the continuing wars of the American West."[24] Through narrative juxtaposition Solnit convincingly submits that imperialist violence of the mid-nineteenth century is cognate with the environmental violence of nuclear testing that poisons and kills Native people to this day, and, given the half-life of such deployed radioactive product, well into the future. Native communities continue to occupy groundzero of U.S. imperialist violence even when their status as the primary victims of imperialism has become ambiguous.

The following account of Yosemite's significance differs from the admirable work of Solnit and Spence in several important ways. First, my interest is to place the episode of Park establishment within a theoretical model of spatial production. While Spence and Solnit imply that their respective accounts merit general conclusions, both have chosen description over the elaboration of a more testable heuristic. My theoretical concerns relate to a second difference from previous work on Yosemite, namely, I emphasize and analyze the manifold productive aspects of the Park. Among these aspects I include the production of value—especially the always surplus valuation of "worthless" land—and the affective intentions and/or results that pertain more directly to the ideological production of American exceptionalism. By this I refer to the Park's place within Olmsted's notions of culture's role in constituting ideal citizens, or, in the terms outlined above, its role in the disaffiliation of various forms of interest and resistance in favor of the category of universalized man, or, republican citizen.

Finally, while Olmsted's biographers have duly noted his involvement with the promotion and justification of Yosemite, the consequential nature of his association has received little more than cursory, and unanimously uncritical (or, I might say, unanimously exceptional) acknowledgment from Yosemite Park historians. Only by scrutinizing the Park's early history through Olmsted's involvement and in the context of his affective philosophy of culture are Yosemite's most important features revealed. These are features, I should add, both within and outside physical geography.

On August 1, 1876, John Muir wrote the following entry describing Yosemite's Lake Tenaya in his journal: "The lake with its rocky bays and promontories well defined, its depth pictured with the reflected mountains, its surface just sufficiently tremulous to make the mirrored stars swarm like water-lilies in a woodland pond. This is my old haunt where I began my studies. I camped on this very spot. No foot seems to have neared it."[25] It is typical of Muir and a common trope of the white man in the wilderness that his arrogant vision erases all history (even, paradoxically, evidence of his own previous visit). Muir's is a kind of possessive rapture that implies the place exists for him; it is his old haunt, he camped here and staked his claim on the study of nature.

The following quote is from the soldier Lafayette Bunnell's *Discovery of the Yosemite and the Indian War of 1851 Which Led to That Event*, wherein Bunnell describes the response of a freshly defeated Miwok leader to a proposed "memorialization" of him and his people:

> When Ten-ie-ya reached the summit, he left his people and approached where the captain and a few of us were halting. . . . I called him up to us, and told him that we had given his name to the lake and river. At first he seemed unable to comprehend our purpose, and pointing to the group of glistening peaks, near the head of the lake, said "It already has a name; we call it Py-we-ack." Upon my telling him that we had named it Ten-ie-ya, because it was upon the shores of the lake that we had found his people, who would never return to it to live, his countenance fell and he at once left our group and joined his family circle. His countenance indicated that he thought the naming of the lake no equivalent for his loss of territory.[26]

I quote Rebecca Solnit at length, for her recent reading of the passage's significance is both concise and eloquent:

> Usually annihilating a culture and romanticizing it are done separately, but Bunnell neatly compresses two stages of historical change into one conversation. Bunnell says, in effect, that there is no room for these people in the present, but they will become a decorative past for someone else's future. Part of what is horrific about this encounter is that Bunnell and the Mariposa Battalion had come to exterminate these native people not out of implacable hatred in the usual spirit of war, but in a blithe administrative way. They were opening the land for economic activity—gold mining, mostly—and the Indians were in their way and had to be removed as the earth above the gold-filled fossil streambeds was, with no more reflection.[27]

Bunnell and the Mariposa Battalion set in motion the historical erasure confirmed by John Muir's representation of his experience in Yosemite.[28] In fact, Bunnell was engaged in a twofold erasure, at once removing the signs of a Native culture and the signs of violence attendant upon the erasure. He was erasing both the Indians and his willed erasure of the Indians. As I will soon explain, no one was more qualified than Frederick Law Olmsted to attest that gold could not, finally, be extracted profitably from the Mariposa Valley and the Yosemite region. The space was, in strict pecuniary terms, of very little value. It is largely for this reason—valuelessness—that within several years of the attack by the Mariposa Battalion Olmsted and other promoters managed to have the region "set aside" as an enormous park. A space of Nature was, as a decisive part of the Park process, further evacuated of history and violence, obscuring imperialism while rhetorically suggesting and materially facilitating American expansion.[29]

Because it is frequently a point of confusion, it is relevant to note here that the fact that Yellowstone, as opposed to Yosemite, is regarded by historians as the world's first national park is the result of a technicality. The 1864 bill signed by Abraham Lincoln set the Yosemite region aside to be managed by the state of California. In 1872, when Yellowstone was established, a similar, and undoubtedly preferred, delegation of management could not be made because Wyoming was not a state. My point is not to set the record straight, but to make clear Olmsted's involvement in the respective moments of park genesis, both urban and national. I will next briefly review the circumstances of Olmsted's departure for Mariposa to highlight issues relevant to the founding of Yosemite Park.

On June 19, 1861, Olmsted's close friend, Henry Bellows, offered him a position as secretary of the newly formed United States Sanitary Commission. Olmsted accepted the offer immediately—he had found the latest incarnation of his "mission." Olmsted's duties with the commission were extraordinarily challenging. He and others fully recognized the threat posed by dysentery, inadequate clean water and decent food, and the generally miserable physical conditions that cost lives and corrupted morale among Union soldiers and officers. The Sanitation Commission was charged with ameliorating what were, finally, insuperable problems. What limited success the commission achieved, especially in the care of the wounded, was hampered, according to Olmsted, by the incompetent administration of resources and delegations by men in Washington. Olmsted, who was loathe to tolerate perceived incompetence among superiors, resigned from his position with the commission in August 1863.[30]

Olmsted left the commission to accept a job from absentee owners as the manager of the gold-mining Mariposa Estate. The estate was a seventy square mile principality at the foothills of the Sierra Nevada Mountains near the Yosemite Valley. It contained around six villages or mining camps populated by about seven thousand people (mostly men), a heterogenous mixture of black and white Americans, Mexicans, Chinese, Indians, and Europeans.[31] In the months before Olmsted arrived Mariposa was producing at a very profitable rate of about one hundred thousand dollars a month in mined gold, though by the time of his assumption of duties production was down about seventy-five percent and promised to go even lower.

Olmsted was heavily in debt when he was offered the job, and the terms of ten thousand dollars a year plus stock shares valued at fifty thousand, and a house, were attractive factors. Olmsted also had the advantage of forming an "insider" relationship with the Mariposa Company's largest investor, banker Morris Ketchum. Ketchum offered to manage Olmsted's stock shares if Olmsted would inform him of Mariposa's financial situation before Olmsted released official reports. This relationship financially benefitted both men, though the Ketchum firm would fold in 1865 for forging checks to finance gold speculation (*PFLO* V: 57-9). Gold in Mariposa, of course, would have saved the firm, but the estate did not produce.

Whatever Olmsted's pecuniary motivations, he justified his departure from the East according to the familiar terms of "mission." In fact, in a letter to his father written while deliberating the offer, Olmsted casts himself as a kind of well-compensated missionary by rationalizing that his influence in the region may be "favorable to religion, good order and civilization. . . . As the clergymen say when a rich parish bids for them against a poorer, I think the call to California is a *clear* one if not as loud as that to the battle here."[32]

Olmsted's friends, especially Henry Bellows, implored Olmsted to stay in the East, arguing that his energy and vision would be invaluable for the rebuilding of a national sense of unity that would be required after the Union's nearing victory.[33] Olmsted retorted that his abilities were overestimated: "I do not think that I am as wise as you allege by a great deal, but I am less influential, my advice and my information are of less effect than I feel they deserve to be—very much."[34] And, as I have already suggested, there was for Olmsted the work of building civilization on the frontier. I cite this dynamic intercourse because it reveals the degree to which Olmsted's definition of himself, his ambition, and his values were brought out as he wrestled with his decision. Contrary to his disclaimers above, Olmsted held an extraordinarily high opinion of his abilities and his personal character, yet the history of his professional endeavors betrays frustration and, not infrequently, failure. In fact, throughout his life Olmsted was plagued by a sense of his inadequacy because of his limited formal education, his seeming lack of consistency and career direction, and what he cites as a string of either limited success or outright collapse: "I have done a good deal of good work in my way too but it is constantly & everywhere arrested, wrecked, mangled and misused & it is not easy for me to get above intense disappointment & mortification."[35]

By departing the East he at once left the location and reminders of his failures, or, at the very least, his perceived lack of influence, and he left the opportunity to perform in the challenging national rebuilding already being planned by the high-profile circle of reformers of which he was a member. Olmsted must have regarded it as a fault of character that he was leaving (however denied) for pecuniary reasons. Olmsted could not help but wonder if there was substance behind his facade; it is not surprising that when he traveled to the West he traveled into a severe personal crisis. His personal crisis, the details of which I will elaborate in what follows, had a counterpart in the crisis of labor and production on the estate. Soon after he arrived Olmsted realized that the projected profits from the mines were grossly overstated. A lode that had brought high returns at the time of purchase was all but played out and attention to infrastructure had been sacrificed for quick progress—the restoration of mines and equipment would require a great deal of money. Olmsted cut wages shortly after he grasped the questionable viability of the estate. Cutting wages precipitated a general strike by nearly all daily wage employees. When the strike turned violent Olmsted had warrants issued for the arrest of "ringleaders" (*PFLO* V: 203-04). One striking worker had, according to Olmsted, "been busy spreading the rumor that I swindled the laborers on the Central-Park & have been sent here to play the same game." Olmsted concluded threateningly: "He will soon leave these parts" (*PFLO* V: 205). Of course, the rumor was accurate; it was precisely Olmsted's record of making the "worst class" of workers labor for the lowest possible wages that led the owners of the Mariposa Estate to recruit him as manager.

The strike ended in its third week, Olmsted having conceded to not a single demand; nevertheless, when he took his departure two years later the estate would be in financial and structural ruin—income was simply too low to meet costs of operation and improvement.[36] What Olmsted took away from his experience was an increased sense of failure, and, more importantly, a "civilizing mission" closely tied to the only success that offered some redemption for his time and efforts in California, the formation of Yosemite Park.

Near the end of the strike Olmsted stated the following in a letter to his father written during a trip to San Francisco: "I am enjoying this visit to S.F., meet many pleasant people and a strong contrast to [Mariposa]. I hate barbarism & like civilization in all its forms. I wish I could live in England. This reminds me that I have often requested Mary O [Olmsted's half-sister] to get me a copy of H Bushnell's Discourse of Barbarism the first danger. . . . I will give $10 or $20 for a copy if necessary" (*PFLO* V: 207). Olmsted described the evidence of poverty among the workers at the estate as a kind of barbarism, a term with cultural and *biological*, or evolutionary, inflections that functioned to racialize class differences. At the moment he was increasing their poverty and putting many out of employment altogether, he was willing to pay dearly for Bushnell's twenty-four page tract. Like Olmsted, Bushnell conceived the frontier less as a safety valve than a threat to republican institutions because it promoted moral and social atavism, and, ironically (though this is unstated by Bushnell or Olmsted), the evidence of the strike suggests that it promoted cross-cultural/racial class solidarity (something Central Park also at once did and interfered with).

Following the writings of John Stuart Mill on the subject, Bushnell saw vagrancy and the general lack of stable community institutions as symptoms and promoters of self-interest, greed, and social irresponsibility.[37] This fact suggests that Olmsted used the idea of "frontier" to refer both to geographic and social conditions, the latter inflected,[38] as later theories of social recapitulation would make clear, with the idea of temporal progress. Thus Olmsted could write to the Unitarian minister Edward Everett Hale that he was unsure which of the "two slants toward the savage condition is most to be deplored and to be struggled with, that which we see in the dense quarters of our great cities and manufacturing towns or that which is impending over the scattered agricultural population . . . of the great West."[39] As cultural historian Robert Lewis attests, it was the perceived possibility that the United States would be, or would continue to be, identified by its barbarism that began Olmsted's own theorization of class difference and his perceived role as a writer and a builder of public spaces in America.[40]

The very first public space Olmsted proposed building in California was a "Reading and Coffee Room at one of [the] mining camps" (*PFLO* V: 213). The room was to be well stocked with British and American periodicals, including the *London Illustrated News, Lloyd's Weekly, Leisure Hours, Mining and Smelting Magazine, Harper's Weekly*, and *Scientific American*. Olmsted explained the purpose of the British journals in a letter to his friend and business partner Edwin Godkin: "The reason for taking so much cheap English stuff is that we want to draw off a considerable number of Cornish miners from the dram shops and gambling booths" (*PFLO* V: 214). As Olmsted's friend Henry Bellows wrote of the urban park, the coffeehouse was made to "teach and induce habits of orderly, tranquil, contemplative, or social amusement."[41] Olmsted proposed the coffeehouse within a few weeks of the end of the strike; it was intended to avert any similar disruption, as Peter Stallybrass and Allon White's analysis of the rise of the coffeehouse in Britain helps to suggest.

According to Stallybrass and White the coffeehouse in Britain became an important social institution during the national crisis of the Civil War. In the context of a radically shifting social order the coffeehouse functioned to mediate the transition from a system of power vested in the aristocracy to one ostensibly more democratic. At the same time, and in the service of the new "democratic" order, the coffeehouse was an instrument of socialization toward middle-class habits and values against the threat of too much democracy. It was an institution to regulate the masses prone to drink and general (libidinal) insubordination:

> The coffee-house thus combined democratic aspirations with a space of discourse less contaminated by the unruly demands of the body for pleasure and release than that of the tavern. The coffee-house was one of the places in which the space of discourse was being systematically decathected. Intoxication, rhythmic and unpredictable movements, sexual reference and symbolism, singing and chanting, bodily pleasures and "fooling around", all these were prohibited in the coffee-house. The emergence of the public sphere required that its spaces of discourse be de-libidinized in the interests of serious, productive and rational intercourse. Not least of course because sobriety and profit hung together.[42]

Having just cut wages and after being physically threatened by the resulting violence (he received frequent death threats), Olmsted proposed a space designed to make the mine employees more sober and professional (hence the subscriptions to mining periodicals).[43] Cutting wages and forming the new public space of the coffeehouse were two aspects of his management toward profit, and, at the same time, the latter was elaborated as a promotion of civility central to Olmsted's nationalist ideal of an exceptional America. Olmsted theorized this America in a "literary" project he never completed: "The Pioneer Condition and the Drift of Civilization in America."

3. "Civilization" and Hysteria

> In the actual scale of the regulated conquest of land . . . [the] persistent image of the invading barbarians is understandable. But the harder fact, that these barbarians were well-born Englishmen, is characteristically displaced.
> —Raymond Williams, *The Country and the City*

In his analysis of the literary representation and effects of English enclosure procedures that despotically organized land and disrupted stable agrarian communities, Williams does not dwell on the complex, ambiguous figure of the "well-born" barbarian. But this figure offers a useful point of departure for discussing Olmsted's personal abjection, and it provides another perspective for understanding his ideas about barbarism and civilization. The reversal Williams offers, where popular or "low" cultural forms represent the upper- or middle-class Englishman as a barbarian, can demonstrate the close relation of Olmsted's personal crisis and his social theories when the elements that form the basis of such a reversal are applied to the relevant context of the Mariposa region in the middle nineteenth century. In this context the crucial "reversing" perspective belongs to the Miwok and other Native peoples violently displaced by the agents of "civilization" interested, primarily, in the mining of gold, or, more abstractly, the production of value. Thus, a recently suggested translation of the Miwok term from which Yosemite was derived—Yo-che-ma-te—as, "some among them are killers,"[44] referring to white men, offers some evidence for the validity of the analogy. It is my assertion below, and the basis of my meaning for the term "abjection," that Olmsted *shared* the Miwok's perception, and, however he managed partially to repress this knowledge, Olmsted understood that he too was, according to the very criteria he elaborated, barbaric.

One of Olmsted's responses to abjection was hysteria, or the manifestation of somatic symptoms stemming from the repression of traumatic knowledge.[45] Olmsted was not passive in the face of his symptoms. In fact, he very actively pursued a course of treatment that was, evidence below suggests, effective. His prescription was the experience of Nature in Yosemite. Combining his reformism with personal treatment, he promoted the establishment of Yosemite Park on the basis of the capacity of landscape to relieve the psychological stresses of modern life. To the degree that Yosemite "healed" Olmsted, it effectively repressed his traumatic abjection. To the degree that Olmsted connected barbarism with the "lower" classes and cognate "races," Yosemite Park was intended as an exceptionalist design, reflecting and constituting an ideal identity while repressing the confusion, personal and social, of classes.

In the unfinished notes for "The Pioneer Condition and the Drift of Civilization in America," Olmsted makes much of the transience and domestic insecurity (the terms used to denigrate and "racialize" Seneca Village in Central Park) of men as a primary cause and symptom of "barbarism." "How many times have you taken up a new business and failed in it since you came to California," Olmsted asks one man soon after he arrived in Mariposa: "'I have been dead broke six times.' And how many times have you changed your business? 'I'm sure I can't tell; I always change when I see a better chance.'" Olmsted concludes that a "few weeks afterwards he made another change and leaving the part of the country where I was, I lost sight of him" (*PFLO* V: 653).

Olmsted complains that despite the presence of a social infrastructure of schools, churches, and hospitals,

> the people are very strikingly more shifting and consequently shiftless
> than those of any part of the Eastern states or of Europe. Since I have

been here (two years) the District Attorney's office has been twice vacated by resignation and is now filled by the third incumbent. The two leading lawyers in the county have left it; four other lawyers have changed their residence. . . . Ten men of my acquaintance who were running mills of various kinds (saw, grain and stamp), when I came here, have left them. . . . The Justice of the peace; the seven successive school-committeemen; three out of four of the physicians; the five butchers; the five innkeepers, eight out of twelve of the tradesmen and their assistants; the blacksmith; the two iron-founders; the two barbers; the daguerrotypist; the bathing-house keeper; the seven livery; the three principal farmers; the three school-teachers and about seventy out of a hundred of the miners and laboring men who have lived nearest me or who most readily accessible and observable to me, have moved from one house, office or shop to another, or have left the county within two years. (*PFLO* V: 655)

Olmsted's scrutiny of the micromovements of his neighbors smacks more than a bit of obsession. They are movements, he claims, that lie "in natal character of the population," who naturally "break loose from the opportunities and the duties in which they have become established" (*PFLO* V: 656). In steadiness, according to Olmsted, is the source of civilization: "Thus civilization requires men to forecast carefully the course by which each can best serve others and to keep steadily to that course; hence one of the chief distinctive habits of the civilized man is that of providing for himself by a sustained and prearranged method of providing something for others. Hence men who live in an uncivilized manner within a civilized community are termed vagabonds or vagrants, that is wanderers who do not provide for themselves by any fixed or sustained method of providing something for others" (*PFLO* V: 665). Olmsted associates the "vagabond" with lower classes and immigrants when he writes that such people came "largely from [Europe's] dangerous classes, mainly from its poorest classes and the more useless of its poor—little from the gentle and educated and highly civilized classes, and scarcely at all from what are called its upper and ruling classes, that is to say, the recognized leaders of civilization" (*PFLO* V: 664).

The sore roots of Olmsted's obsession with steadiness are easily exposed. His own biography reveals a vagabond, marked by repeated failure, frequent movement and anxieties about his usefulness to other people and especially to his own family. He began his adult life as a "gentleman" farmer, but when he was unable to turn a profit he took up journalism, performing in this capacity his extensive Southern traveling and newspaper publishing. Later he invested in a publishing house that shortly failed, precipitating his minor nervous breakdown. While Olmsted was recovering at a resort, the job of Central Park superintendent was offered to him.

He left his Park duties willingly, though amid some controversy, at the start of the Civil War to manage the new volunteer Sanitary Commission. Unable to form a good working relationship with others tied to the commission, Olmsted left, eventually for California to manage the Mariposa Estate. His departure from the Sanitary Commission severely strained Olmsted's relationship with his father, who expressed great impatience at his son's unsteadiness. John Olmsted's letters do not survive, but his hostility may be inferred from those of Frederick to his father. It is clear that a lack of faith in his son had been growing: "You seem to give yourself unnecessary annoyance by adding to your regret that I was no longer able to keep the [Central Park] post, regret for my incompetence, weakness and folly. . . . It pains me that you should have the misfortune of supposing me to be so much less respectable a man than I am" (*PFLO* IV: 613). In fact, Olmsted referred to himself as a "vagabond" on several occasions, as in the letter to his father from Mariposa from which I quoted above: "I reduced wages on the 1st & all hands on the estate are on strike since. They tried a mob but made nothing by it. . . . I shall hold out till they come to my terms and dismiss all who have been prominent in the strike. . . . I am at present making money pretty fast for such a vagabond as I am" (*PFLO* V: 206-7). This is the same letter where he expresses his wish to live in England. While producing the conditions that qualify Olmsted's notions of barbarism he implicates himself and those very terms, and, as one might expect, his wish to get away is what limits his recognition of the contradiction.

As several of his critics and/or biographers have confessed, failure and unsteadiness are the chief characteristics of the greater part of Olmsted's life.[46] Olmsted appears entirely unaware of the irony, though the repressed returns in the form of his obsession with local movement and his constant battle with various forms of anxiety. On Christmas Day 1863 he writes the following to his friend Henry Bellows:

> With Mariposa and what I have here I am greatly disappointed. . . . I feel like an old man setting about planting oaks—or as if I had got a very heavy burden upon me and could see no place ahead where I could back up for a while and rest. I really am not well and strong. I don't know what's the matter, but one queer thing is certain, I am pen-sick. I no sooner get pen to paper than a horrid sort of night-mare begins to grow upon me, and the longer I write the worse it gets, till finally my eyes twitch and I have to quit to avoid suffocation. (*PFLO* V: 165)

Olmsted had a history of what were contemporaneously described as hysterical symptoms, including temporary paralysis, episodes of blindness, frequent head-aches, fainting spells, and severe depression. In the above case, Olmsted's hysteria is brought on at the scene of writing because during this period he is continuously confronting another looming failure, that of the Mariposa Estate, which is repeatedly the subject of his reports to friends and employers. In taking up the pen he must bear witness to his own failure and unsteadiness, to, finally, his own "barbarism," to the ambiguity of his own social status and inevitably racial identity. Writing brings home his projection and denial and fills him with horror. In his "Notes" Olmsted enters a short parable that renders explicit what is at stake in his painful effort to maintain his "civilized" identity. Olmsted introduces the parable with a reference to Mayhew's *London Labor and London Poor*, specifically Mayhew's reduction of human diversity to "two distinct and broadly marked races, namely, the wanderers and the settlers—the vagabond and the citizen, to nomadic and the civilized tribes":

> I believe this in the main to be a true statement and that a similar division may be made of every so called civilized community. Every now and then we may find in an Eastern society an Indian who lives peaceably and industriously, who has adopted the usual fashions and manners of the community very closely and who respects and obeys the laws as a good citizen. Yet those who know this man thoroughly are generally aware that the Indian propensities and habits remain and are really stronger than usual with him because of the prolonged suppression to which they have been subject. Occasionally in a furtive, solitary way he gives rein to them. After a time, in many cases, he will suddenly, at what appears to be a great sacrifice, abandon whatever he has gained as a citizen, part from his friends, make his way to the frontier or to some other opportunity for escaping from the restraints of organized society and for the indulgence of his independent, vagabond, deep seated proclivities. (*PFLO* V: 659)

This is a nearly perfect description of the circumstances of Olmsted's departure for California. Here Olmsted becomes the Indian, the barbarian, in his own script of America's prospects for civilization. Stallybrass and White have written about the politics of displacement and metaphorical sublimation, how it "is in fact the main mechanism whereby a group or class or individual bids for symbolic superiority over others: sublimation is inseparable from strategies of cultural domination."[47] Sublimation is a slipping of social and psychological metaphors at once, involving complex denials and projections deployed unconsciously in bids for power. One of Olmsted's principal reasons for going to California was his sense of a mission to bring civilization to the frontier, to replace barbarism with civility. I am suggesting that his concealed mission was both self-regulation, or ideal constitution—the repression of ambiguity—and social domination. On the individual level the move to California exhibits the contradiction representative of Olmsted's complex and fractured identity. He is both barbarian and agent of civilization, the understood habits of the former denied and displaced even in the moment of their enactment: Olmsted, the vagabond salesman of stability. Contemporaneous use of the term "vagabond" most frequently associated it with Native Americans who either had not "adopted the usual . . . manners of the community" or who were mixed race. One writer wrote approvingly of the effects of an Indian boarding school: "I had seen miserable vagabonds on the frontier; but the civilized, scholarly, Indian boy and girl presented a new sight."[48] Anxiously anticipating an attack by Utes, a frontier military surgeon described an "old medicine-man—an unusually malevolent looking old vagabond" inside the frontier fort where the surgeon was stationed.[49] Another writer reported from Yosemite about the presence of "vagabond half-breeds."[50] Olmsted himself employed the term with a racial inflection, as when he dramatized his experience of camping in Texas in 1852 with the following: "who knows what wild-cat, wolf, or vagabond nigger may be watching to spring upon you if you go further from the light."[51] Olmsted, by his time in Mariposa, may have been anxious that he had strayed too far from the light. The contradiction erupts in obsession and neurosis, not to mention the production of parks.

On the social level the contradiction is not quite so apparent; or, more exactly, Olmsted's historical agency is played out more clearly in the broad operation of power. No psychological conflict changes the fact of certain material transformations and realities. Olmsted lowered wages and forced people out of work (in both Central Park and Mariposa) and though this was done in contradiction to an often repeated desire to raise the standard of workers' lives, the fact of the contradiction does nothing for the strikers who lost their jobs. Andrew Carnegie precipitated the same contradiction on a grand scale at Homestead some years later. Like Carnegie later, Olmsted built public spaces to obscure *substantial* contradictions, namely, those of class difference and spatial devaluation. Olmsted's role in the formation of Yosemite Park is important for such reasons.

Olmsted made his first trip to the Yosemite Valley, about a one-day ride from the border of the Mariposa Estate, with his family in the summer of 1864. He wrote repeatedly to family and friends in the East of his physical response to the region and the incomparable nature of the Yosemite environment. The following, from a letter to his father, is typical:

> The Sierra peaks are generally of a light grey granite though some are of slate. Their form is that of snow-drifts after a very gusty storm, some being of grand simplicity while others are pinnacled, columnar castleated and fantastic. [Though I cannot truly] attempt to convey to you any

impression of the scenery which is of a very peculiar character and
much the grandest that I have ever seen. I gained health constantly while
in the mountains, felt better and could ride further without fatigue than
before for a long time, but I find the old symptoms returning as soon as
I come back to the desk. (*PFLO* V: 253-56)

Nature as a cure for neurasthenia is a common theme of Olmsted's work and
the work of various promoters of natural space in the nineteenth century, and
certainly even to this day. The face of Nature presented Olmsted with no evidence
of failure or contradiction; in fact, Nature was the antithesis of contradiction: the
very absence of human presence and history assured a scene evocative of timeless-
ness and stability. Yet such an idealization still required some scene of writing, as
Olmsted clearly demonstrates in the same letter to his father: "As there was no
evidence that one peak had ever been ascended by men before, we took the usual
privilege and named it Mount Gibbs, in respect to Prof. Gibbs of Cambridge"
(*PFLO* V: 256).

No anxiety attends the abstract nomination of geography because it is principally a gesture of erasure, exclaiming no human history in the very act of inaugura-
tion into imperialist history. Olmsted's healthful and exuberant naming is the
counterpart to Ten-ie-ya's experience of loss suggested by Bunnell. In his diary
Bunnell suggested that name Yosemite itself was a form of the Miwok word
Uzumati and translated as "grizzly bear," referring, he believed, to the Indians'
perception of the men of the Mariposa battalion. More recently, Alfred Runte has
claimed that Yosemite is a corruption of Yo-che-ma-te. As I mentioned earlier, it
is a term still likely referring to the battalion, and probably white men in general,
and is translated as "some among them are killers."[52] The space of the Park could,
emphatically, be the scene of natural history, but of human history there was to be
no presence. The Indian, according to Olmsted's understanding of the Native's
vagrancy and penultimate "barbarism," was a dire threat to the healthy civilization
that the landscape of Yosemite promoted. Thus, Olmsted writes in "Notes on the
Pioneer Condition," the "Indian met with on the frontier is the antitype and the
natural enemy of the civilized man. . . . According to the civilized standard he is a
lazy, ravenous, brutal, filthy, improvident, lying, treacherous, blood-thirsty scoun-
drel" (*PFLO* V: 685). Olmsted generalizes the character of the Indian to represent
a "class" that afflicts all communities, and he proposes cultural institutions as the
crucial agent for reforming, or civilizing, such a class:

These miserable, demoralized, drunken, diseased, abandoned wrecks of
the feebler sort of savages, are and always have been by thousands a
part of the population of all those communities wherein the authority of

government and all the machinery of law, and many of the institutions of civilization—churches, schools, newspapers—have been, after a sort, established, and which lie immediately in the rear of those where the war with the Indians is still kept up in a more or less intermittent way. (*PFLO* V: 688)

Olmsted thus places Yosemite Park directly "in the rear" of the Mariposa Battalion's war against the Miwok.

In the "Preliminary Report upon the Yosemite and Big Tree Grove" that Olmsted composed as commissioner of the new Park, he sets forth several principles for governing the Park and justifying its existence; a central assertion involves the profit of individual health:

> It is a scientific fact that the occasional contemplation of natural scenes of an impressive character, particularly if this contemplation occurs in connection with relief from ordinary cares, change of air and change of habits, is favorable to the health and vigor of men and especially to the health and vigor of their intellect beyond any other conditions which can be offered them, that it not only gives pleasure for the time being but increases the subsequent capacity for happiness and the means of securing happiness. The want of such occasional recreation where men and women are habitually pressed by their business or household cares often results in a class of disorders the characteristic quality of which is mental disability, sometimes taking the severe forms of softening of the brain, paralysis, palsy, monomania, or insanity, but more frequently of mental and nervous excitability, moroseness, melancholy, or irascibility, incapacitating the subject for the proper exercise of the intellectual and moral forces. (*PFLO* V: 502)

Generalizing from his own experience, Olmsted slips quickly from a celebration of the benefits the Park offers the individual to suggestive warnings about the dangers of general inefficiency and demoralization that can affect all people without the luxury of Nature: individual health is a metonym of national health. In his complex paranoia over the spectre of barbarism, Olmsted is drawn to claim a hierarchy of influence that inflects his theory with a desire not only to have Nature provide a particular service to the middle class, but also to differentiate himself from the savage: "The power of scenery to affect men is, in a large way, proportionate to the degree of their civilization and to the degree in which their taste has been cultivated. Among a thousand savages there will be a much smaller number who will show the least sign of being so affected than among a thousand persons taken from a civilized community. This is only one of the many channels in which a similar distinction between civilized and savage men is to be generally observed" (*PFLO* V: 503).

Olmsted dances around a contradiction that he manages to resolve so as to relieve his abject anxieties. If scenery had the "power" to affect all men equally, *but that not what you quote him as saying* and if the Miwok and other Yosemite peoples were such long inhabitants of Yosemite's penultimately affective vistas, then the Indians should display a high, if not the highest, degree of "civilization." Of course, Olmsted has reserved for himself, as one of America's prime reformists, the category of civilized. To resolve the problem civilized and savage become essentialist categories. Olmsted largely avoids confronting the contradiction that this, in turn, introduces (i.e., How does scenery maintain its affectivity over essential differences?) and instead simply asserts the profoundly inexact notion of "degree" of civilization and its relation to affect. Olmsted's convolutions reveal what is at stake: his effort to dispel personal abjection, to secure his ideal identity. Yosemite cures him, it represses his constitutional ambiguity, and this is, precisely, the great advantage of Nature: *it reflects and reinforces an idealism that is likewise the foundation of authority.*

In language evocative of republican universalizing bids of Jefferson's "Declaration," Olmsted draws a metaphor suggestive of both violence and national importance: "It is the will of the Nation as embodied in the act of Congress that this scenery shall never be private property, but that like certain defensive points upon our coast it shall be held solely for public purposes" (*PFLO* V: 500). The Park was to defend the middle class, a "species" of "We the People," from the "forces" of degeneration and the hysteria produced by overwork that they may work more efficiently. It was also to help secure a specifically class-based national identity by the promotion of benefits to the cultivated and refined citizen and, in a simultaneous influence of differentiation, identify the savage unimpressed by the landscape of Nature. Without introducing the complexity of Whitman's famous celebration, I can safely suggest that Olmsted's exceptionalist projects intended no democratic vistas. Furthermore, as with Central Park, the pecuniary benefit, the profit made on worthless space, is an essential if obscured aspect of the view from Yosemite. *of what kind?*

I conclude this chapter by suggesting that regarding profit it is significant that it was not Olmsted who first proposed the idea that Yosemite become a reserved space, for all intents the world's first National Park, but Israel Ward Raymond of the Central American Steamship Transit Company. Raymond sent the Yosemite proposal to John Conness, the senator from California, and justified the idea on the basis of the land's lack of value: "The summits are mostly bare Granite Rock. In some parts the surface is covered only by pine trees and can never be of much value."[53] Conness introduced the Park legislation in Congress and declared similarly: "I will state to the Senate that this bill proposes to make a grant of certain premises located in the Sierra Nevada Mountains, in the State of California, that are for all public purposes worthless, but which constitute, perhaps, some of the greatest wonders of the world."[54] The Senate passed the bill into law and immediately selected Olmsted to serve as commissioner since he was in the area and had broad support from his management of Central Park.

Olmsted was hired by the owners of Mariposa Estate to manage a property with great potential value; during his tenure the gold panned out, debt ran high, and the price of the estate's stock plummeted until the property had lost nearly every bit of its value. In the midst of this downfall he was appointed to oversee the management of an adjacent property, Yosemite Valley, that was set aside on the grounds that it had no value. Olmsted was the well-paid manager of vast and worthless lands. On the one hand was the formally corporate space of a gold-mining company, the place of Olmsted's literal office, the scene of his writing and hysteria, and the testament to his failures, instability, and fractured identity—according to his own terms the evidence of barbarism that polluted and withheld the promise of the Nation. On the other hand was the "worthless" space that both symbolically foretold the Nation and facilitated national expansion. As the corporation plunged into bankruptcy the Park arose, a parcel of space initiated by a representative of corporate interest and harboring a manifold promise of profit: health, money, and a purified symbology. Such was the value of worthless space.

The monetary profit that the Yosemite Park can be said to have yielded has many aspects and is at once quite easy and quite difficult to ascertain. Concessionaires were established within Park space even before legislation was passed that officially rendered it a park. The right of these enterprises to remain was never seriously contested, though the business of providing goods and services was eventually to fall primarily to the park service itself. Many millions of people have used various modes of transportation to travel to the Park and the money made by those in the business of providing such transportation has been very great. Capital has been well invested in the infrastructure of expansions that both surround the Park and of which it is representative. In monetary terms it is a categoric fact that Yosemite National Park has proven a fantastic financial success. This fact should not be obscured by the severe funding limits under which nearly all national parks have had to operate throughout their existence; as Yosemite Park displaces history, so it displaces profit.

In Yosemite profit, history, and people were displaced. In the next chapters I develop a theorization of this process of multiple displacements but shift my geographical focus to highlight the financial interest and economic efficacy of the deployment of "nature." By focusing on Yellowstone I am also able to demonstrate more fully how the national park functioned to facilitate the violent appropriation of Native territory. How did Yellowstone become the penultimate American *place* it is today? It had more than a little to do with the need to secure the future of American capitalism.

Chapter Three

The (Over)Production of Place

[W]hen I went to Alcatraz, in my own way it was going back home again.
—John Trudell, *Stickman*

When a group of representatives of various indigenous nations and organizations occupied Alcatraz Island in 1969—to bring attention to the oppressed condition of Native America and assert land claims, beginning with the island—the National Park Service quickly submitted a report to the secretary of the interior suggesting that Alcatraz become part of the Golden Gate recreation area. As one recent historian of the occupation, Troy R. Johnson, notes, "the report did not mention the Native Americans occupying the island."[1] Throughout the nineteen-month occupation, which collapsed, for a number of complicated reasons, the national park idea was frequently proposed by federal and state agencies. The group representing Native interests on the island, Indians of All Tribes, responded to the proposals with the following:

> The government's proposal is nothing more than the formation of another park . . . unneeded, undesired, and actually an attempt to end the Alcatraz movement. . . . The public thinks this is really going to be tribute to the American Indians, but this proposal of the government's provides for a park which will have some supervision by handpicked Indians subjected to government control and then, from then on, Alcatraz will become just another government park. . . . Our answer to the U.S. government that this island be turned into a park . . . at this time, and at any other time, is an emphatic NO.[2]

On June 29, 1970, H.R. Bill 18071 was passed, transferring title of Alcatraz Island to the Department of the Interior. A "top secret" removal plan was soon developed named "Operation Parks"—the Indians were to be baited into violence by the Coast Guard and then an assault force of U.S. Marshals was to take over the island.[3] On June 11, 1971, the marshals went in, met no resistance from only a handful of Indian men, women, and children, and reclaimed federal control of Alcatraz. It is now part of the national park system. Contested territory has become a national monument.

The representatives of American Indian peoples who occupied Alcatraz chose the site for its symbolic value. Occupying an infamous island prison suggested the history of Indians' internment on reservations scattered throughout the U.S. The very reasons the island was chosen to house a prison—its lack of exploitable natural resources, its isolation—were the same criteria used to decide the territory for Indian reservations. It was, the occupiers like Native activist and artist John Trudell believed, an appropriate place to begin the assertion of Native land rights. The park was deployed to defeat the Indians' assertion.

The first chapter took 1857, with its great Panic, as the central "moment" for an analysis of the role of Nature in mediating economic crisis and social upheaval. 1857 was the birth year of the American urban park. 1872, when Yellowstone was established, is, according to technical fact, the birth year of the national park. It was also a year that disclosed early signs of the coming Panic of 1873, an event that would prove the formal start of the longest and most terrible depression to that time in the United States.[4] In 1873 the conservative banking house of Jay Cooke & Co. failed, an event marked as the starting point and causal "straw" of the panic.[5] While even very astute critics of American landscape ideology continue to regard Yellowstone Park as principally the product of a growing preservationist movement—an effort to hold picturesque and sublime Nature from private ownership and commodification—it was, in fact, precisely Jay Cooke, baron and financier of the Northern Pacific Railroad, who instigated the process that led to the park's founding.[6] Cooke developed the propaganda for the park to secure financing for further western rail expansion, when, in 1870, it was an investor's market as far as railways went. Rail bonds were for sale throughout Europe and America for a number of transcontinental lines, and consequently bond buyers were not easy to secure. This was an early sign of the coming depression that began in earnest in 1873—initiated precisely by the overproduction of railroads. The polemical assertion of what follows is that Yellowstone Park was a leading cause of the Panic of 1873 and the consequent depression. This assertion, though, is something of a simplification.

Yellowstone Park was equally an effect of economic crisis. As I recount below, the idea for the park was sold to Congress by promoters working to distinguish Cooke's line from other investment possibilities at a time of tremendous rail overbuilding. As the investment situation became highly competitive, Cooke pushed for expansion in the hopes for profit to see him through the lull (here began the campaign for Yellowstone Park), he overextended, failed, and soon the national economic system crashed. The crash was terrible. The ensuing class conflicts tore the nation and many institutions apart, for a time, and threatened to alter radically the social, political, and economic character of the United States. Reaching a climax in 1877, huge and violent strikes demonstrated that the working class and unemployed would not consent to be governed by a social and political system that could exploit and dispose of people as fiercely as did American capitalism in the 1870s. Here too, in the field of class warfare, I will show Yellowstone Park had a role to play.

While the relationship between the railroads and western expansion has been a common topic of Western studies, only Richard Slotkin has explored significantly the relation of frontier ideology and western expansion to urban crises and conflicts. In the following I am less engaged with his most influential book, *Regeneration through Violence*, than with *The Fatal Environment: The Myth of the Frontier in the Age of Industrialization*, a book which discusses at great length the relation of the "frontier," as myth and an aspect of ideology, to American industrialization and urban crises. In *Fatal Environment* Slotkin does not disown his reading of the cultural expressions of western expansion he developed so brilliantly in *Regeneration*, though the broad and more recent New Age appeal of the Jungian interpretive system he employed has led him away from the archetype toward a sometimes confused concentration on myth *and* ideology (he often neglects clearly to distinguish the two). Slotkin's strength in both of these volumes—which together with *Gunfighter Nation* provide the most sustained critique of the central American metaphors and symbols first skillfully interrogated by Henry Nash Smith—lies in the power of his thesis (violence against Indians as metaphor and means for national economic and cultural revitalization) and his unparalleled ability to interpret accordingly vast amounts of literary, popular, scientific, political, and economic material. Yet, as critics quickly pointed out, Slotkin's central "Frontier myth" is shown to hold so many complicated relations to issues like Reconstruction and metropolitan crises that the principal features of his subject are obscured and confused.[7] While brilliantly disclosing that the West provided the key cultural metaphors for a broad range of nineteenth-century interpretations of regional and national crises, Slotkin inevitably reinforces the myth.

What could help resolve the problem of myth reinforcement is a willingness to recognize the myth's limitations and introduce competing or corresponding ideas and concepts that account for other, if similar, aspects of the ideology that the myth both reproduces and represents. Most importantly, the notion of the West as "Garden" (described and criticized by Henry Nash Smith[8]), should not be subsumed under the myth of the Frontier; the former has its own particular history and usages which, unlike the latter, do not assume conflict as an aspect of their rhetoric. Smith's mistake was to accept, to some degree, the terms of the Garden myth itself and leave undeveloped the theme of conflict; Slotkin's lies in overdetermining a rhetoric openly chartered by conflict. The notion of the West as Garden is enabled precisely by the repression of the violence and conflict that Frontier rhetoric gloriously assumes. It also has a central ideological function of promoting immigration rather than justifying extermination. In myths of the Garden, civilization is not sweeping away barbarism in a bloody but necessary running fight. The symbols of "barbarism" (the Indian, according to the intentional symbology of the Frontier), in fact, if present at all, appear as aesthetic features (in landscape painting or "salvage" anthropology) inseparable from the symbolic epistemology of a space imagined as harboring only resources of pleasure, national culture, or profit. I harbor no desire to reassert the dominance of the Garden myth, which, as I will show, does, finally, represent a great deal of violence; in fact, I will be discussing the ideological uses of both the Frontier and the Garden in what follows. My emphasis is on the agents, the ideological and economic processes, which (or who) elaborated such respective rhetoric to mediate the social and economic crises of the 1870s and on how such elaboration produced a particular geography of exclusion and an important American *place*: Yellowstone National Park.

The problem of myth reinforcement which attends Slotkin's analysis is related to his confusion regarding myth and ideology. The effect of this confusion is to abstract from the economistic interpretation of events and cultural products he seems always on the verge of elaborating. In the following I attempt to correct the problem of reiterating the issue I am criticizing by explicitly relating my reading of economic events and cultural or state endeavors (like western explorations) to American exceptionalism. The issues, rhetoric, and events surrounding Yellowstone are various instances and/or inseparable elements of the production of space and American place, which is in turn about the constitution of idealized American identity, an identity that is marked by the absence of class and is yet profoundly involved in the maintenance of class differences.

Developing the spatial theories of Henri Lefebvre and David Harvey, and combining them with theories of American nationalist identity formation offered (principally) by Lauren Berlant and Priscilla Wald, I will show how Yellowstone Park was involved in the capitalist *production of space* and was manufactured finally as a national symbolic place, working to elaborate the myths and symbols of a national culture and consciousness that in turn perform the hegemonic work of constituting national subjects and producing broad consent. I attempt to trace and to define ideology in a way that does not overdetermine cultural nationalism but seeks to determine how and why cultural symbols are elaborated in the context and with regard to the particular agency of economic figures or processes.

In *The Production of Space*, Henri Lefebvre suggests that when viewed from a certain perspective, or according to a particular thematic mapping, the region of southern France reveals two aspects: "It will be readily seen that this vast area, which has been earmarked, except for certain well-defined areas, for tourism, for national parks . . . is also destined for heavy use by a military which finds such peripheral regions ideal for its diverse purposes."[9] I harbor no wish to confuse the strategic intelligence of the French military's contemporary defensive or aggressive activities around the Mediterranean with American military and political activities in the West over a century ago, but Lefebvre's insight does effectively illustrate one of the themes I will develop here, concerning the *unmapped* violent, imperialist aspects of America's "first" national park. For Yellowstone National Park was formed not primarily as a reservation for nature (its rhetorical justification and explanation from 1832 to the present), but as an important aspect of the devastating appropriation of territory from various indigenous western nations. Yellowstone was a beachhead in the expansion of the United States' economic and cultural domination.[10] In this view Yellowstone is, to repeat, not a space of nature reserved, but at once a socially *produced* space and a consuming and consumed space.[11]

Related to my understanding of the matter of consumption, Karl Marx explains that "commodities are the elements of capitalist production, and commodities are its product; they are the form in which capital re-appears at the end of the process of production."[12] According to a capitalist system, all geographic space is a product precisely through its status as a commodity: property has value and can be bought and sold. Despite the existence of contesting social and economic systems that may not recognize the abstraction of value applied to land, a capitalist system, and certainly the one that unfolded in the United States, could tolerate only the assumption of such an abstraction.[13] Violence is an inevitable and particular sign of two fundamentally opposed systems of territorial conception in a single, though often quite vast, space. In the history of the American West violence signifies the *production of space*, to use Lefebvre's terms. It is a sign of imperialism where imperialism itself is regarded as constituted spatially in the effort to bring resources and markets under the social and economic control of the state and its capitalist interests.[14] Production in this sense is formally different from the traditional

Marxist formula, where it is, as Marx writes, "considered as the unity of labour process and the process of creating value."[15] Although an infinite amount of labor may occur in a particular space, a space can achieve value with no application of what we usually regard as labor. Space only needs to have been *mapped* into the capitalist network for it to have value and be open to exchange.

Lefebvre, in all of his work, develops his principal thesis that the spatial ordering of society is a crucial means for controlling threatening social contradictions and that it invariably serves hegemonic interests.[16] Thus the interest of the state in spatial order: "Space has become for the state a political instrument of primary importance. The state uses space in such a way that it ensures its control of places, its strict hierarchy, homogeneity of the whole and segregation of the parts. It is thus an administratively controlled and even policed space."[17] Any space outside the network of value and unavailable for exchange exists in contradiction to any social order based on private property. In a very real sense it is no space at all, or an *unproduced* space, lacking any status as a commodity. At the moment such a space becomes the *object* of capital expenditure it enters to some degree into the status of a socially *produced* space. That this status may be achieved through a great deal of contest is readily evident in any glance at imperialism in action. One definition of imperialism then, is to say, as I have already, that it is the *production of space*. At the same time it is important to remember that production is not always profitable and that certain forms of production may precipitate conflicts and contradictions more threatening than those displaced. In fact, it is precisely *overproduction* that is most frequently described as the origin of most major nineteenth-century economic crises.[18]

In descriptions of social and economic crises rooted in overproduction the role of space is left unconsidered or, if it is considered, it is suggested as an aspect of crisis resolution: expanding the territory of the productive network opens new markets for proliferating goods and absorbs enormous amounts of surplus capital.[19] Surplus is expended and created *at once* in the tenuous contradiction that characterizes capitalist development. Nowhere is this more evident than in the extension of the technology of transportation across the American West in the nineteenth century. Yellowstone National Park was both a result of such extension and a principal instrument of the imperialist process. And, true to the contradictions of nineteenth-century U.S. capitalism, it was involved in both the effort to resolve economic crisis and in the precipitation of that crisis.

In my analysis of the people, processes, and events within and surrounding Yellowstone, in the fused dimensions of history and space, I hope to contribute to an understanding of the material conditions and the realm of affect of the elaboration and production of the "national symbolic."[20] I offer an analysis of nationalist efforts to establish a particular, which is to say exclusive, identity for the country and its (incorporated) people that pays close attention to the economic context and agents with regard to such efforts. What I reveal is not economic determinism so much as a rich ideological process that does not obscure financial trends and events by overdetermining the rhetoric of cultural nationalists, who may have been directly employed by the era's principal capitalists in propaganda efforts to increase the value of particular assets—like western land.

For instance, in what is otherwise a valuable essay, Patricia Hills provides an example of cultural overdeterminism: "To . . . nationalistic and forward-looking gentlemen, expansion was a prerequisite to America's destiny as an international leader. Cultural nationalism became a necessary corollary. Culture, that is, the arts, had a role to play in this destiny by actively strengthening allegiance to the American Union and encouraging commitment to the course of future expansion."[21] Hills is postulating a false distinction between nationalistic gentlemen and artists, and though she is, to be sure, suggesting their ideological similarities, she is finally describing a conceptual tautology; the artists she is interested in (Bingham, Stanley, Bierstadt, and others) were nationalistic, forward-thinking gentlemen; meanwhile she neglects the complex financial incentives for expansion that benefitted from and clearly lay behind expansionist thinking. Defining cultural nationalism by reference to cultural nationalism is really no definition at all. Defining it dialectically with economic processes, while being constantly wary of reductionism, has the great benefit of providing some materiality for understanding.[22] /

As I will show, Yellowstone Park was sold to the U.S. Congress and, some evidence suggests, the American "citizen" (English speaking, white, and relatively privileged) by Jay Cooke as he faced the prospect of the substantial capital devaluation of his assets. Cooke failed (for a time) financially—the western expansion he sought for the Northern Pacific Railroad was precisely what ruined him—but he was at least successful at commissioning a revived symbology of Nature in the guise of public recreation. That is, he financially supported the elaboration of potent and longstanding American attachments to Nature: physical and spiritual health and redemption, adventure and self-reliance, individualism and prosperity. For Cooke Nature was a complex symbology to be mined for financial profit, if not directly by him, at least at his investment. ?

The ideological connection between economics and psychology is suggested by the term "national symbolic," which I borrow from Lauren Berlant, who, in her study of Hawthorne and the nation defines it as "the order of discursive practices whose reign within a national space produces, and also refers to, the 'law' in which the accident of birth within a geographic/political boundary transforms individuals into subjects of a collectively-held history."[23] In this case the "law" to which

Berlant refers is that of the Lacanian Symbolic imposed on the unconscious. Lacan writes: "The unconscious is that chapter of my history that is marked by a blank or occupied by a falsehood; usually it has already been written down elsewhere. Namely: in monuments . . . in archival documents . . . in semantic evolution . . . in traditions, too, and even in the legends which, in a heroicized form, bear my history."[24] Reading Berlant's Lacanian reference alongside her reference to space presents the analogy between the material geographic and the unconscious. The law that "fills" the unconscious is drawn from the "space" of the nation, leading us to realize that the production of national space is essential to the production of national subjects. The spatial dimension Berlant refers to is crucial, though more complex than she suggests.

Ideally, according to exceptionalist ideology, the national symbolic operates within a particular material (in addition to psychological) geography to provide the unconscious structures of personal identity roped fast to the real and invented nation. As I will describe in more detail in what follows, I am referring to the psychological aspects of the meaning of *place*, expressing an ineradicable *lived* relation to a particular geography. In nineteenth-century America the actual geography the nation sought to control was not entirely the nation's place, but had to be produced as such. It was the *place* of others, particularly indigenous peoples, lacking, as I have tried to suggest, even the status of space for the purposes of the American nation and economic system. I am suggesting a two-staged transformation, from a native place to a principally capitalist space (manifold economic resource), and from capitalist space to national place, a species of what Berlant calls the national symbolic.

The transformation from indigenous place to capitalist space is recorded in many ways, one of the most obvious being acts of landscape nomination and another being the actual violence of war. But the production of such space is an incomplete though necessary aspect of the nation's use of a particular geography. Its larger interests lie in the reproduction of its citizenry, a goal achieved in the "monuments" of the unconscious which cannot be established on the thin soil of mere space. The Symbolic goal of the production of space is the subject of place, the individual consenting to national identity. Thus the nation would constitute all of its geography as place—a powerful and constitutive rhetoric of national ideals, though one that did not go uncontested.

Which is to say that the social and cultural productions that compose the national symbolic, certainly in the case of "places" like Yosemite and Yellowstone, are not merely a rhetoric or even politics of nationalism. Instead, they are acts of territorial dispossession that at once destroy identities contrary to national interests and gain the space for the unfolding and domination of a particular economic system. Throwing oppositional peoples and cultures into turmoil amid processes inseparable from the economic interests of particular capitalists, the state and capital at once combine to produce national monuments designed to constitute Americans. In acts of genocide and dissolution they invent a spatial rhetoric of unity, a national symbolic place, like the national park.

In penetrating and wide-ranging analyses of how a national(ist) "people" is constituted, Priscilla Wald writes that,

> an official story of "a people" invariably lags behind the seismic demo-graphic changes and corresponding untold stories that ultimately com-pel each revision. A national narrative must make the concept of a "home" for "a people" appear intrinsic and natural rather than contin-gent and, ultimately, fictive. At the same time, the narrative must make the concept of home able to accommodate both changing and contested frontiers and the mobility within its borders. "Home" must be suffi-ciently elastic to incorporate the local into the national.[25]

(Anderson?)
(Anderson
no Anderson)

Wald, who focuses on the literary "negotiations" and artistic innovations of writers as varied as Frederick Douglass and Gertrude Stein—who write largely, if com-plexly, "outside" the consensual narratives they creatively negotiate—develops concepts of particular value for critical efforts aimed at the disclosure of many aspects of the national "official story," including those repressed. "Official sto-ries," Wald asserts, "constitute Americans." And they are infinitely malleable, changing "in response to competing narratives of the nation that must be engaged, absorbed, and retold."[26] Thus, even Justice John Marshall's 1831 verdict denying Indian national sovereignty within the United States by at once asserting depen-dency and foreclosing citizenship is a telling moment in the complex negotiation of "constitutional" national narrative. In this case preserving contested conceptions of property and barring the troubling spectre of an "imperium in imperio," reflect-ing America (with all the exceptionalism that hegemonic term implies) only with an uncanny difference. In Homi Bhabha's terms, "almost the same but not white."[27]

What Wald repeatedly asserts, without specifically developing, is the double aspect of the endlessly flexible official story: its narrativity is bound to place. Her emphasis on *story* does not blind her to geographic factors, but it does inhibit aspects of an analysis that an examination of place can disclose. Lefebvre writes: "What is an ideology without a space to which it refers, a space which it describes, whose vocabulary and links it makes use of, and whose code it embodies?"[28] Americans are constituted by geographies in which hegemonic narratives are inscribed. The official story is embodied in national symbolic places, that are, inevitably, crucial points of ideological negotiation and resistance. Thus, when the

[handwritten marginalia: Why does Russell Means piss + queer frequent Central Park, while everyone else is evidencing to way of one's own installation "Harbor" or another?]

American Indian Movement activist Russell Means pissed on the sculpted faces of American national icons at Mt. Rushmore in 1970 he was protesting a narrative embodied in place and asserting a counternarrative which held the same geography as part of a much different story.[29]

As Means has noted, the 1970 protest and occupation took place in an "official" national monument, Mt. Rushmore, and the use of such monuments and parks as tools of expropriation was often discussed and publicly denounced by the occupiers: "[Lee Brightman] spoke [to the media] about Teddy Roosevelt, the biggest thief ever to occupy the White House. Roosevelt violated scores of treaties, and illegally nationalized more Indian land than any president, before or since. He called his booty 'national parks' and 'national forests' to cement the thefts into law."[30] Official stories are rhetorics (visual, spatial, or verbal) intended to gain the consent, which is to say, "Americanize," the massive diversity of peoples who occupy the geographic boundaries of the United States. Clearly, they sometimes fail.

[handwritten marginalia: Slide as transitive verb?]

While, as with the above, I will be pointing out particular failures of "constitution" in what follows, such is not my principal concern. I will describe the processes by which a place is constituted. By sliding the application of this term, "constituted," away from the prospective governed and onto the locational "story" itself, I reveal less the unofficial stories of those attempting to negotiate or resist the national narrative than the "unofficial" story (or, to stay with my metaphors and concerns, space of "silence") of the material processes and agents that/who both enable the narrative and are excluded by it. Who or what produces a national symbolic place? Besides the ideological intentions (manufacturing identity, a geography of exclusion [with racial implications] and an exceptionalist consciousness), what are the economic factors and interests? Who is to profit? In a manifold sense, who or what is to be redeemed, and how? My conclusions suggest that mediating the ruptures of national unity that occur along the fault line of class is the principal function of the constitution of national symbolic place in the American West. Toward the end of this chapter I develop latent themes from the previous chapters on the connection of the spatial history and rhetoric of the urban park with the "frontier" park. Constituted places in the business of "constituting Americans" at once obscure and elaborate class difference while producing *value* for America's "redemptive" capitalism.

Studying Yellowstone and the West adds a layer of complexity to my analysis of Nature and exceptionalism, or the double preservation and "erasure" of class difference, because of the involvement of a heterogenous mass of people and nations, namely, American Indians, who are not directly subordinate to capitalist employers or interests. There is some evidence, to which I will return, which suggests that some Indian people were articulated by white reporters and intellectuals according to terms frequently applied to the urban "lower" class. What is unambiguous is that producing space in the West functioned, though with a great deal of contradiction, as a "spatial fix" for capitalism, one that segregated native people and, by the logic of the geography of exclusion, contributed to their elaboration as racially inferior, or, as Olmsted had it, "barbaric." Of course, the Indian reservation has since become the location of much of the nation's worst poverty and social conditions so that the geography of exclusion has rendered race and class indistinguishable.[31] In the following I attempt to respect this complexity, but I focus primarily on the details of spatial production and the role of Yellowstone in both mediating and precipitating economic crises that made class conflict an obvious threat to capitalists in urban areas. In this case, Yellowstone functions to absorb various surpluses of overproduction and constitute identity in a manner similar to Central Park.

Chapter Four

The Nature of Violence: Crisis and Redemption in Yellowstone National Park

"Enit?" Chess asked. "What are you?"
"Shit," Simon said. "I'm a Communist. A goddamn pinko redskin.
Joe McCarthy would have pissed his pants if he ever saw me."
—Sherman Alexie, *Reservation Blues*

In America a sort of idealized and conspicuously nonviolent space had long been objectified as a scene by various promoters of American real estate and westward expansion. Witness William Penn's seventeenth-century rendering of the Pennsylvania landscape (fig. 1). Penn announces the American landscape as a model of the ideal British countryside.[1] A great deal of open space is interrupted by occasional clumps of towering, shade-giving trees. The land appears ready-made for planting or leisure, and what is more, seemingly free for the taking.[2] In an advertising strategy precisely the same as that to be employed by Jay Cooke about two hundred years later, Penn extols climate and bounty in the accompanying text: "The place lies 600 miles nearer the sun than England ... which is about the latitude of Naples in Italy, or Montpelier in France." Timber, fish, fowl and "wild deer" are reported to be plentiful.[3] More immediate precedence, with regard to this study, for the idealization of the American landscape came from gentlemen explorer/artists like George Catlin who left the following vision of the western territories after his journey by steamer to the mouth of the Yellowstone River (fig. 2).

Violence was not frequently chosen as a subject of landscape painting, especially when the intent of such paintings was promotional, though Thomas Cole, the central figure of American landscape art at the time of Catlin's journey, poeticized, "All was harmony and peace—but man / Arose—he who now vaunts antiquity—/ He the destroyer—amid the shades / Of oriental realms, destruction's work began."[4] However, as art historian Angela Miller has noted, Cole's actual "view" of American destructiveness was highly ambivalent.[5] This ambivalence is evidenced in part by his completion of *The Oxbow* the same year as the pessimistic *Course of Empire* (1836). The former well-known painting depicts a wilderness foreground with a dominant pastoral background and a storm retreating across the landscape. The violence is at once signified and removed.

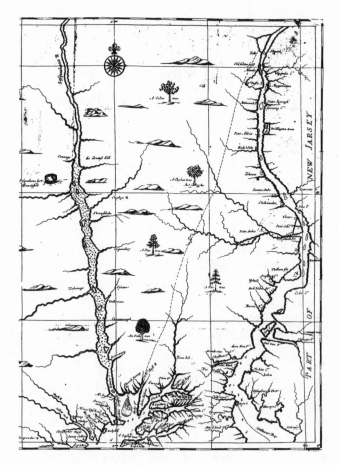

Fig. 1. William Penn's Promotional Map. *A Map of some of the South and East Bounds of Pennsylvania in America*, by John Thornton and John Seller, London, 1681. Reprinted from Richard S. Dunn and Mary Maples Dunn, *The World of William Penn* (Philadelphia: University of Pennsylvania Press, 1986), 44.

In fact such paintings as Catlin's *Beautiful Prairie Bluffs*, or Coles's *Oxbow* are, to an important degree, representative of the visual rhetoric that effectively obscured violence in the nineteenth century. As the following demonstrates, war surrounded the "production" of landscape and landscape art, most obviously in Catlin's case. Which is to say that what requires some explanation is how such a picturesque landscape, particularly the western landscape, is produced out of the bloody historical context of the Indian wars. The following passage from Catlin's *Notes* belies the context: "In my former epistle I told you there were encamped about the Fort a host of wild, incongruous spirits. . . . Amongst and in the midst of them am I, with my paint pots and canvass. . . . My easel stands before me, and the cool breech of a twelve-pounder makes me a comfortable seat, whilst her muzzle is looking out at one of the port-holes."[6]

Fig. 2. George Catlin, *Beautiful prairie bluffs above the Poncas*, 1832.

Catlin renders synonymous the eye of artist and the muzzle of the cannon, directing our understanding that the idealized landscape is to be realized through war:

> The operations of my brush are *mysteries* of the highest order to these red sons of the prairie . . . who all meet here to be amused and pay me signal honours; but gaze upon each other, sending their sidelong looks of deep-rooted hatred and revenge around the group. However, whilst in the Fort, their weapons are placed within the arsenal, and naught but looks and thoughts can be breathed here; but death and grim destruction will visit back those looks upon each other, when these wild spirits again are loose and free to breathe and act upon the plains.[7]

Watching Catlin sitting upon his cannon and painting a landscape where the Indians themselves are reduced to minuscule figures in the foreground of a fantastic stylized geography would strike them as mysterious indeed. The incongruity between Catlin's confidence in the mimetic transparency of his art and the perceptions of his subjects who, in the mid-1830s, represented a very powerful military force, is remarkable.[8]

Yet, whether he was prophetic, overconfident, or delusional (which his hyperbolic prose suggests), Catlin made no mistake about the terms of what was to become a very protracted conflict. The cannon beneath his ass, or, according to position, between his legs, was to glow hot.[9] Yet, George Catlin is an important figure not only for his work as prophet and painter of an Ideal West, but for being the first to articulate the idea of a specifically *national park*:[10] "what a beautiful and thrilling specimen for America to preserve and hold up to the view of her refined citizens and the world, in future ages! A *Nation's Park*, containing man and beast, in all the wild and freshness of their nature's beauty."[11] Catlin, in this famous articulation, maintains his fortified perspective. In fact, the principal function of the park is ambiguous, intended both to preserve a "wild" environment and to separate firmly the refined and civilized from the beasts. The language suggests strong delimitations: nature becomes a "specimen," "held up" as an object (or scientific resource) for the "refined," "containing man and beast." The "park," according to Catlin, is thus an aggressive effort to control space, or, more exactly, to transform a particular space of imperialist violence into a space variously useful as a nationalistic device and scientific or recreational resource.

Catlin's work and ideas reveal some important points about the ideological origins of American wilderness "public" space. Not only is the notion of a national park attached to spatial control and racialist segregation, it is clearly inseparable from the conventions and symbology of American landscape painting. This is one of the principal reasons why the signs of violent history (even to this day) are nearly impossible to detect in Yellowstone and other "wilderness" parks. From the moment of conceptual inception our view has been aestheticized. We see "nature" as a picture of Nature, with all the cultural and ideological conventions this *not at* implies, including representations symbolic of national values and the erasure of *Devil's Tower* conflict. Gina Crandell's assertion is correct: "nature has come to be seen as a *Junk* particular type of object, symbolized by a view that can be pictured. . . . [P]ictures influence, and perhaps even help constitute, our perception of places."[12] Thus, Catlin suggests a national park not to preserve some "fading" cultures, animals and geography, *as such*, but as a kind of enormous landscape painting announcing national greatness through the aesthetic symbology suggestive of limitless resources, freedom, adventure, and, most ironically, peace. In short, Catlin was far less a preservationist than a producer of ideas and representations of a national symbolic place. Yet, one of the reasons it would take some forty years to realize an actual national park was that the region had not yet been socially *produced*.

1.

Well before the explorations of Lewis and Clark, the Yellowstone area had first entered capitalism's productive network as a source of beaver pelts. The region's fur trade peaked around 1830, but the animals were exploited to unprofitability by 1850. It was not until 1860 that the first military expedition, under the command of Captain William Raynolds, entered the Yellowstone region. As historian William H. Goetzmann writes, "The initial impetus to military exploration in the high plains and mountain area of the present-day Dakotas, Montana, and Wyoming was the threat of a general Indian uprising by discontented bands of Sioux Indians being pushed ever westward toward the hunting grounds of their traditional enemies, the Crows, by the increasing pressure of white emigration into the northern plains and Rockies."[13] Raynolds's expedition took place about six years after the Great Sioux war had begun, if we assume a starting date suggested by historians like Goetzmann, who see the war initiated by the Sioux with the killing of Lt. J. L. Grattan and twenty-nine other soldiers on August 19, 1854.[14] Regardless of the official date of the conflict, Raynolds's expedition expresses the first serious federal interest in the area.

Captain Raynolds was trained as a soldier and topographical engineer. He had seen limited action in the Mexican War and was anxious about the demands of his new commission to the Yellowstone region, which was to describe "as far as practicable, everything relating to . . . the Indians of the country, its agricultural and mineralogical resources . . . the navigability of its streams, its topographical features, and the facilities or obstacles which the latter present to the construction of rail or common roads."[15] Thus the first state-sponsored intrusion into the area (Lewis and Clark traveled to the north) was assigned to map and gather logistical information for use in an ongoing war against the Native nations in and around the region and to map for prospective railroads. Consistent with the processes of socially produced space the act of mapping was also the act of appropriation, as evidenced by Raynolds's introduction to his official report, which he assembled in Detroit in 1867. Regretful that he was not able to enter the upper Yellowstone Valley, Raynolds explains that had his "attempt to enter this district been made a month later in the season, the snow would have mainly disappeared, and there would have been no insurmountable obstacles to overcome. I cannot doubt, there-fore, that at no very distant day the *mysteries* of this region will be fully revealed, and, though small in extent, I regard the valley of the upper Yellowstone as the most interesting unexplored district in *our widely expanded country*"[16] (my empha-sis). If Catlin imagined the Indians perceiving his art as "mysterious," presumptu-ously assuming ignorance in a people long accustomed to the use of paints for symbolic purposes, here Raynolds associates the term with the geography and people he failed to map for the logistics of war. In fact, he *exclaims* possession precisely because he failed to *claim* possession by the act of topographical inscrip-tion. Here *mystery* signifies an anxious failure to *produce* space and it inevitably compels the verbal rhetoric of inevitable possession.

With the exception of various gold seekers, the Civil War distracted organized attention from the Yellowstone region, though stories of its "mysteries" trickled out and seeds of the coming flood of tourist and railroad interest were often planted by the press. Thus the *Helena Herald* in 1867: "A few years more and the U.P. Railroad will bring thousands of pleasure seekers, sightseers and invalids form every part of the globe, to see this land of surpassing wonders."[17] A combination military and private expedition was planned for 1869, but the Indian War required the soldiers elsewhere and frightened all the civilians away but three; their explora-tion has come to be known as the Folson-Cook-Peterson expedition. The stated purpose of this foray was to take some account of the "tall tales" the region in-spired; the expedition reintroduced the rhetoric of preservation, though it made no call for a park. Camping at what is now called Bridge Bay, Folsom wrote the following:

> This [bay] was about one thousand yards across and was nearly reefed. Large flocks of geese and ducks were feeding near the shore or floating gracefully on its smooth surface. Beyond the lake the timber was tall and straight and to appearances as thick as cane in a southern swamp.

This was one of the beautiful places we had found fashioned by the practiced hand of nature, that man had not desecrated. . . . It is a scene of transcendent beauty which has been viewed by few white men, and we felt glad to have looked upon it before its primeval solitude should be broken by the crowds of pleasure seekers which at no distant day will throng its shores.[18]

Effectively preserving the compelling "exotic" that the rhetoric of mystery serves, Cook, out "exploring" (mapping) the region, simply transforms the mystery in kind. Sublime visual contrasts, like those familiar to landscape painters, denote the "practiced hand of nature," a characterization that revealingly confuses the agency behind the visual invention. Catlin proposed that nature, in Yellowstone, be a painting, and so it appears to be. The mystery of unmapped space is now the mystery of "transcendent beauty." Coincident with the acts of spatial production is the elaboration of a *place* already pictured according to the symbology of an idealized America.

Years later, at a national park function in 1922, Cook credited his expedition with formulating the idea, if not quite precisely, of a park: "[One night in camp] I said that . . . something ought to be done to keep settlers out, so that everyone who wanted to, in future years, could travel through as freely and enjoy the region as we had. . . . None of us definitely suggested the idea of a national park. . . . But we knew that as soon as the wonderful character of the country was generally known outside, there would be plenty of people hurrying in to get possession, unless something was done."[19] The national park as a national place is articulated as a decommodification of *space*, an idea which strikes as absolutely contrary to the social and economic operations of capitalism, rejecting as the idea does the principles of private use and property, not to mention the potential of profit. The national park, according to such rhetoric, would appear to lie outside the space of production. And yet, the private members of the Folson-Cook-Peterson party were not in fact the first to make publicly the case for a Yellowstone National Park: this honor would go to a representative of Jay Cooke's Northern Pacific Railroad, Nathaniel P. Langford.

After a Hawthornian fashion, in the spring of 1870 Langford lost his job as collector of internal revenue for Montana and an appointment as governor due to a dispute between the U. S. Senate and President Johnson.[20] In June he met with Jay Cooke in Philadelphia; there they conspired on the usefulness of Yellowstone exploration in the grand scheme of Northern Pacific Railroad publicity.[21] Langford had found a new job, though at the beginning of a period of desperate conditions for American railroads and for Jay Cooke's enterprises in particular.

The 1860s had been a boom time for American railroads and capital accumulation led to an overproduction of rail miles from 35,085 to 70,651 between 1865 and 1873.[22] Here overaccumulation was invested directly in the geographic expansion of the system of transportation. As Walter LaFeber writes in his invaluable economic history of American imperialism in the later nineteenth century, railroad expansion was tied to the desire to relieve general surplus production of goods. In particular, a transcontinental railroad was considered an important development toward the opening of the vast Asian market.[23] But, in this case, overproduction was no cure for the ills of overproduction. Between 1870 and 1877 average railroad earnings (not profit) per mile dropped from $9,000 to $6,381. In 1874 the earnings from operation for the Northern Pacific were only $365,343—this amounted to $22,876 above expenses; soon Jay Cooke and the Northern Pacific declared bankruptcy and the railroad went into the hands of a receiver.[24]

The conditions for the rampant railroad failure are described by historian Slason Thompson:

> The large receipts per mile previous to 1871 had furnished the stimulus for the over-construction of unproductive mileage which swept scores of railways into bankruptcy during the business stagnation that attended the restoration of our currency to a sound money basis following the return to specie payment on January 1, 1879. An examination of the reports of the leading systems that went into the hands of receivers in 1874 reveals the fact that their difficulties proceeded from one of two causes—either they were in process of construction involving the raising of large sums before they had begun to earn sufficient revenues to pay operating expenses; or their income was so depleted by the reduction of rates . . . that the cost of operation absorbed too large a proportion of their earnings.[25]

The Northern Pacific was an example of the former. It was at the start of a sharp devaluation slide when Jay Cooke pushed for the declaration of Yellowstone as a national park in 1870-71. Overproduction had led to geographic overexpansion, which predictably contributed to the deep financial crisis that seemed irreversible by 1872 (over 150 railroads would seek the protection of courts between 1873 and 1880[26]). As in 1857 overproduction was general, but the railroads represented the most heavily overfinanced industry: "Every line of industry had been stimulated beyond its needs in anticipation of still greater profits. Borrowers went heavily into debt . . . to develop new industrial enterprises with the inevitable consequences of over-production. . . . Railroad building had come too fast to be healthy."[27] Under the impression that greater expansion would see him through the hard times, Cooke sought to promote Yellowstone and the promise of tourist revenues as a means of gathering more expansion financing. Langford's 1870 expedition was for the purpose of such publicity.

In the late summer of 1870 twenty men, organized by Langford, were assembled for an expedition. However, similar to the earlier scare, rumor that the Crows were "on the warpath" left only eight willing to "risk their scalps" by the time of departure. Langford, nervously attempting to enlist the experienced adventurer James Stuart shortly before departure, wrote the following: "I am just d____d fool enough to go anywhere that anyone else is willing to go, only I want it understood that very likely some of us will lose our hair."[28] Stuart replied that, "From present news it is probable that the Crows will be scattered on all the headwaters of the Yellow Stone [sic], and if that is the case, they would not want any better fun then to clean up a party of eight. . . . It will not be safe to go into that country with less than fifteen men, and not very safe with that number. *I would like it better if it was fight from the start; we would then kill every Crow that we saw, and take the chances of their rubbing us out*" (my emphasis).[29] Stuart would be unable to engage in this shoot-first policy, though he did, finally, agree to go with the party, and in fact lead it. "Unfortunately," he was called to jury duty shortly before the planned departure; he claimed that he could not be excused. Langford wrote later that, "our subsequent experience in meeting the Indians on the second day of our journey . . . and their evident hostile intentions, justified in the fullest degree Stuart's apprehensions."[30] The surveyor general of Montana, General Henry D. Washburn, replaced Stuart.

The support of General Washburn led to a last-minute approval of military escort and supplies—thus the expedition combined the representatives of one of the nation's most powerful capitalists and the U.S. military. Besides Langford and Washburn the roster represented various interests of state and capital: a Montana judge, Cornelius Hedges; a civil engineer and president of the First National Bank of Helena, Samuel T. Hauser; merchants Warren C. Gillette and Benjamin Stickney; and two federal revenue assessors, Lynn Trumbull and Truman C. Everts. Among the unnamed in Langford's description were various soldiers and two black cooks; among the former was Lieutenant Gustavus Cheyney Doane, a central participant in one of the most horrible massacres in Western history; it occurred the previous January.

The Marais River massacre was part of an army effort to eradicate the Blackfeet. Under the command of Major Eugene Baker 230 men left Fort Ellis on January 6, 1870; according to Doane's biographer, the

> force marched thirteen days in the dead of winter, with temperatures dropping to 44 degrees below zero, to attack a Piegan camp of Bear Chief and Big Horn on the Marais River (in present day north central Montana). At 8:00 A.M. on January 23, Doane, commanding Company

F, led the attack in which 173 Indians were killed: ninety women, fifty children, and thirty-three men.[31]

It is striking that the biographers give the details of the weather immediately before the body count, as if the massacre were some excuse, or even reward, for frostbite. What they only imply, through body count, is that the Blackfeet warriors were out of camp—the men killed were mostly elderly. No one in the camp was able to offer resistance. One U.S. soldier was killed and one wounded. Doane's own account of the affair is likewise remarkable in that it utterly avoids the issue of nonresistance and commends the bravery of certain soldiers in avoiding friendly fire:

> The First Sergeant . . . deployed his men properly and at a run, and in two minutes the Indians were completely surrounded. The other companies came up in a few minutes, and commenced firing, which was continued for an hour. During this time the First Sergeant kept his line effectively, having with him Sergeant Moore and about twelve (12) men. They were in great danger, as the dismounted cavalries were firing in their direction constantly, and they were obliged to maintain an exposed position in order to cut off the Indians who endeavored to break through the lines. Not an Indian got through though several were followed high up on the slope of the opposite Bad Lands, and killed with revolvers. . . . Corporal Etheridge distinguished himself in killing Indians, taking great risks by standing in front of the lodges and firing into the doors.[32]

The massacre was motivated by a public outcry that the American Fur Company trader Malcolm Clark had been killed by the Blackfeet on August 16, 1869. In fact, he had been killed by a Blackfeet Indian, one of his own relatives by marriage, in a family dispute.[33] In 1889, near the end of his busy military career, which included being first on the scene of Custer's defeat, Doane applied for the job as Yellowstone National Park superintendent. Advertising his credentials, he wrote that he was the "first and last man in Piegan camp January 23, 1870 [during the] greatest slaughter of Indians ever made by U.S. Troops."[34]

It is possible that the details of horror could obscure my principal point: the prodigious violence against indigenous peoples was not peripheral to the production of the landscape of America's first national parks. Violence, as I have been asserting, is a means and marker of capitalist spatial production, or the transformation of a nonproductive space, a nonspace, into a productive *space*. The Washburn-Langford-Doane expedition held principal agency in this transformation: the production of capitalist space.

For American capitalism such space must be produced; for the Native people it was the *place* of their lived lives. Raymond Williams, an excellent though infrequently recognized theorist of place (Heidegger gains far more attention), discusses its significance in *Resources of Hope*, where he analyzes his own writing of his reaction to the death of his father in *Border Country* and *People of the Black Mountains*.[35] Williams's description resonates profoundly with Native American experience:

> It was very difficult not to see [my father] as a victim in the end. I suppose it was this kind of experience which sent me back to the historical novel I'm now writing . . . about the movements of history over a very long period, *in and through a particular place in Wales*. And this history [of Wales] is a record of . . . defeat, invasion, victimization, oppression. . . . The defeats have occurred over and over again, and what my novel is then trying to explore is simply the condition of anything surviving at all. . . . It's the infinite resilience, even deviousness, with which people have managed to persist in profoundly unfavorable conditions.[36] (my emphasis)

Williams adds that a "new theory of socialism must now centrally involve *place*. When capital has moved on place is more clearly revealed."[37]

By Williams's understanding, place is more than a particular geographical area; it is, in a dialectical fashion, produced by and productive of the identity of the people who inhabit a region. As Williams describes it, *place*, existing prior to the violence of capitalism's production of the area as space, survives somehow with the transformation, is itself certainly transformed, but maintains its significance through the survival of the people with whom it is intimate.[38] In fact, Williams suggests that, against a rationalist separation of people and land, *place* signifies the inseparability of a people with the geography of their lived lives. In addition, it is likely that a recognition of the concept of place, let alone its theorization, would be impossible without the ontological crisis of spatial conflict—the violence of the capitalist production of *space*.

Williams helps refer to an apparent contradiction in my use of the concept of place. For Williams, and for the Blackfeet and Crow of the northern Rockies, loss threatened place in the tide of imperialist violence that sought to produce space and, finally, a national symbolic place, or landscape. Place is what constitutes identity, which is why having a particular geography function only as a capitalist space is insufficient—national identity must be constituted to secure social stability and consensus. Thus the national symbolic is pounded out of the material of the local. Constituting place is an act involving the concealment and revelation of the violence of spatial production propelled by the effort to resolve (in the case of Yellowstone) financial crisis.

What was soon called the Washburn-Langford-Doane expedition was the most important expedition to the area because, as I will show, it led so directly to the formation of Yellowstone National Park; further, it represented several aspects of capitalist and military interests in the territory (including the representatives of enormous violence), interests which affected the production of space and national place—the two aspects often operate simultaneously within a capitalist order.

According to the 1851 Treaty of Fort Laramie a great deal of what was to become park territory was described as the central portion of the territory of the "Crow Nation." According to this treaty the reservation encompassed over 38 million acres.[39] In 1868 settler interest in the land led the commissioner of Indian affairs, N. G. Taylor, to request a smaller reservation: "The Blackfeet and Crow nations claim much the larger portion of the [Yellowstone] Territory, and there can be no question but that it would be for their interest, as well as for the benefit of the citizens of Montana to yield their title and be restricted to tracts of country of much less extent yet sufficient for their need."[40] The result was the second Fort Laramie Treaty of May 7, 1868, by which the extent of the reservation was reduced by about three-quarters.[41] Though much smaller, the reservation still contained the majority of what was to become Yellowstone Park in the state of Montana. It was at this time that the Washburn-Langford-Doane expedition explored the territory. The result of their expedition was Langford's systematic promotion of the area.

Under the law signed by President Lincoln on July 2, 1864, the Northern Pacific received the greatest land grant ever given to a railroad, some sixty million acres; the bill also contained "several minor amendments, among them one binding the government to extinguish the titles of Indian tribes to lands embraced within the area of the grant."[42] The grant followed the Yellowstone River and led directly through Crow and Blackfeet reservations, though it did not directly overlap what was to become park territory. In a handwritten plea for federal subsidy of the railroad, Jay Cooke argued that his road would "invite and encourage immigration and the colonization of a country now an unpopulated waste. It would help to solve the Indian question and promote civilization generally. It would afford means for the transportation of soldiers and supplies to the forts and government posts on the Frontier."[43] Cooke solicited the opinion of General Hancock about the "Indian question," and Hancock replied that "[the railroad] will most probably provoke [Indian] hostility, especially that of the Sioux, and lead to a war ending in their possible destruction."[44] Cooke sought the extinction of Native land claims, if not the Natives themselves, and promoted his railroad as the precipitator of transformation and war.

Langford's expedition and hired promotion of the region was accomplished to secure popular *and* financial interest in the area of Yellowstone in order for Cooke to sell bonds for railroad construction at the highest possible price during the start of a major financial crisis rooted precisely in railroad overexpansion. Such overexpansion left Cooke with a difficult money raising project, as evidenced in a letter from his close business associate, H. C. Fahnstock: "I can't for the life of me get up your enthusiasm in the Northern Pacific, chiefly I suppose for the reason that at every step here I am confronted by the experience of others who have bonds to sell and cannot place them. . . . People have much faith in your ability. . . [but they] argue a man may be poor with uncounted acres of land. . . . You are confident at popularizing the bonds. To do this you must show a sure way to earn at least the interest."[45] As Fahnstock makes clear, the problem with Cooke's western land assets was their lack of productivity—while the land grants may have begun an incorporation and transformation into capitalist space, the area was hardly fully *produced* or productive. The double meaning of Fahnstock's last sentence—both advising Cooke to propaganda efforts (public interest) and reminding him that he must assure profitability (financial interest)—precisely discloses the crucial economic meaning of Yellowstone Park.

With so much railroad expansion up for sale, Cooke required some distinction in his own route that would yield a profitable sale of bonds. That distinction was Yellowstone and the principal publicist was Langford. Besides the sheer necessities for the promotion (financial pressures), a nagging problem was that the territory Cooke hoped to make profitable was largely occupied by Nations at war with the United States. Thus, a requirement of Langford's publicity would be a demonstrable absence of Indians and violence in the region. It was necessary for Cooke to advertise according to a reiteration of landscape tropes I considered earlier, rather than a fighting adventure, because he wanted both tourism to Yellowstone and permanent landholders along the entire western route of the railroad. Cooke drew from the landscape symbology of peace, independence, and endless resources in his particular deployment of American exceptionalism.

2.

The Washburn-Langford-Doane "explorers" frequently engaged in a common and seemingly utterly irresistible habit: they climbed to the tops of mountains. The purpose of the act was manifold. They climbed to gain and enjoy the aesthetic view (to see Yellowstone as painting); to chart the land as part of their topographic enterprise; they did it to confirm their identity as explorers; and they did it to erase history. From a distance the landscape absorbs any sign of habitation. Raymond Williams suggests this prospect in his novel *Border Country*, where the protagonist climbs a local mountain and finds his familiar community transformed. At one level he knew that it "was not only a place, but people, yet from here it was as if no one lived there, no one had ever lived there. . . . The mountain had this power, to abstract and to clarify."[46] While sociobiologists may theorize a human proclivity for high ground is an evolutionary taste of a properly defensive character, it is likewise an act of metaphoric domination and erasure. At the top of a mountain there is room for but one body; in assuming the summit all others disappear. Contrary to Foucault's theorizing, such an ultimate panoptic position is ontologically constitutive: to observe is to *be, alone,* no one else in sight. Such was one means of denying Indian presence in the territory of the national park. There were others.

In Langford's *Diary* of the expedition Indians appear as a kind of phantom, or "mysterious," presence, just ahead or just behind the party, only once actually seen, with all signs of Indians disappearing entirely by about the midpoint of the journey. Thus, on August 23, Langford writes that fresh "Indian signs indicate that the red-skins are lurking near us, and justify the apprehensions expressed in the letter . . . I received from James Stuart, that we will be attacked by the Crow Indians. I am not entirely free from anxiety. Our safety will depend on our vigilance." On the 25th they spot what they think is a smoke signal of Indians scouting their party, and on the 27th Langford writes that they "think the Indians cannot be far from us at this time." But other than a distant sighting on August 23, Indians never appear. (It is likely that the Indians were retreating from the incursion.) By September 15 Langford no longer expresses anxiety about attack (even for dramatic effect): "We have seen no sign of Indians following us since we made our first camp upon the lake, and but little evidence that they have ever been here."[47] Even this evidence was soon to disappear altogether.

By the time Langford published the story of his Yellowstone "adventure" in *Scribner's Monthly* in May of 1871, he could write that his "journey . . . continued through a country until then untraveled."[48] This article, "The Wonders of Yellowstone," was explicitly intended as publicity for the Northern Pacific.[49] Set in a hyperbolic tone of daring adventure it mentions Indians only initially and briefly for dramatic effect.[50] As the title suggests, the focus is on the fantastic geographic features of the region, from the picturesque ("From [the hill's] summit we had a beautiful view of the valley stretched out before us—the river fringed with cottonwood trees—the foot-hills covered with luxuriant, many-tinted herbage"), to the natural sublime ("The brain reels as we gaze into this profound and solemn solitude [of the Great Falls]. We shrink from the dizzy verge appalled, glad to feel the solid earth under our feet").[51] In this context the Indians are reduced, as in Catlin's painting, to natural features, living curiosities meant to evoke feelings of threat, danger, and wonder (the stereotype of the Indian is a figure "profound and solemn") but who should in no way challenge the right of the tourist/adventurer to travel and gaze freely. The Indian is at once present and absent, there (only in small numbers) but staking no claim to either power or territory. Barbara Novak rightly asserts that the "reduced" figure of the Indian actually functions to *empty* the landscape in American paintings. The absence of white or European figures in nineteenth-century American landscape painting is, she writes, "loaded" with meaning: "Man has not yet entered Eden. Sublimity belongs only to God. We know that the idea of creation—of a primal and untouched nature—had an immense resonance for the American psyche. The uninhabited landscape amplifies this thought." This, as I previously suggested, is the mountaintop view. But, according to Novak, "one type of figure can be introduced into this landscape without disrupting this—the Indian, who, as a function of Nature symbolizes its unexploited state."[52]

Elaborating the "insignificant" (i.e. powerless, with no claims to ownership) Indian presence, Hiram Chittenden, who, in 1895, composed the first history of Yellowstone National Park, offered the consensus opinion when he wrote that "it is a singular fact in the history of the Yellowstone National Park that very little knowledge of that country seems to have been derived from the Indians."[53] He goes on to declare that the available evidence "clearly indicates that this country was *terra incognita* to the vast body of Indians who dwelt around it."[54] One of his proof texts is Doane's military report from the Washburn expedition; Chittenden quotes the following:

> Appearances indicated that the basin [of Yellowstone Lake] had been almost entirely abandoned by the sons of the forest. A few lodges of Sheepeaters . . . wretched beasts who run from the sight of a white man, or from any other tribe of Indians, are said to inhabit the fastnesses of the mountains around the lakes, poorly armed and dismounted, obtaining a precarious subsistence and in a defenseless condition. We saw, however, no recent traces of them. The larger tribes never enter the basin, restrained by superstitious ideas in connection with the thermal springs.[55]

The idea that Native presence was at best tenuous and temporary, or that what people there were constitutionally degraded, as if bound to extinction, forms the very center of European justifications for acts of genocide since the Columbian era. Attached in the Colonial era to the epistemology of natural philosophy, the settlers held that proof of Native inferiority was evidenced in their greater susceptibility to disease. They further justified Native extermination by subscribing to a monogenist theory of human origins, which led to the inevitable fact that the Indians migrated here (possibly even as the lost tribe of Israel) and could therefore have no greater claim to the territory than the colonists themselves.[56] While Doane's and Chittenden's ideas are certainly inflected with this history of pseudoscientific naturalism, the monogenist/migrationist view had given way to notions of civilization versus barbarism tied to anxieties of national identity. Of course, according to the newer, "scientific" views the Indians were no less degraded and so their presence in future national space was no more tolerated. One way of pretending they were never there is represented by Doane's suggestion that the Indians were afraid of Yellowstone's "wonders." The mysteries, or, "superstitions" Doane both resolves and perpetuates are exploited in a rhetoric of humiliation and degradation that absurdly exclaims Indian absence in the very paragraph that notes Indian presence.

Occasionally, the statements by those involved in Native dispossession belie the presence that so much effort went to obscure. Thus, park commissioner George Wingate in 1886: "The Indian difficulty has been cured, the Indians have been forced back on their distant reservations, and the traveler in the park will see or hear no more of them than if he was in the Adirondacks or White Mountains."[57] Mark David Spence puts together extensive evidence against the notion of Indian absence. He writes that, to those involved in the rhetoric of erasure, "it mattered little that the first word of Yellowstone came from the various tribes of the Rocky Mountain region, or that evidence of Indian camps could be found throughout the geyser basins."[58] It was ideologically necessary that there should be little sign of Indians.

In fact, archaeological evidence of Native habitation in the region dates from the end of the last Ice Age. Indian oral testimony reveals that the geyser region was a common site for vision quests.[59] But, whatever the evidence of long-term occupation, including numerous discoveries of artifacts and camping sites, the presence of actual Native inhabitants around the era of exploration in the 1870s was impossible to ignore.

Various branches of the Crow and Blackfeet nations lived in the area of Yellowstone Park as part of their migratory living patterns around 1870. In fact, Langford records evidence of a controlled burning, probably done by Crow, he came across during the 1870 expedition. But, as Spence writes, "the Native groups with the longest connection to the Yellowstone area at the time of its 'discovery' . . .were a loose association of bands that anthropologists broadly refer to as the Eastern and Northern Shoshone."[60] A closely related people residing in Yellowstone at the time were the Bannock, one division of which was pejoratively referred to as the "Sheepeaters" by white explorers (as in Doane above). In fact, the Tukudika, contrary to Doane's description of their pathetic and beastly condition, were described by an earlier trader as "all neatly clothed in dressed deer and sheepskins of the best quality and seemed perfectly contented and happy."[61] There is a great deal of evidence to suggest that by the 1860s and 70s the area that was to become Yellowstone National Park was being used more heavily by various Indian groups than in the past, due to the pressures of settlement, which pushed Indian peoples from lower regions and food sources to the elk herds of these higher altitudes.[62]

Still, the park region was repeatedly described by Langford and other promoters as a vast, beautiful, and vacant space, to be reserved from private exploiters for the pleasure of all people. Geography was imagined as art. The particular nineteenth-century American tradition of landscape representation, from the Hudson River School, including Bierstadt and Thomas Moran, to travel narratives and military reports, idealizes the "natural" space such that national progress is represented as inevitable through the receding image of the Indian figured as part of the iconography of the picturesque, and diminishing to be figured not at all. Recently, Ken Burns's film, *The West*, once again elaborates such visual rhetoric. Burns's black-and-white images—many drawn from Edward Curtis, the famous photographer of Native Americans—appear between the inevitable shots of a beautiful, expansive, and emphatically empty American West. The images of the Indians, stylized by Curtis to evoke a sad longing conducive to a retrospective assurance that a culture has died, obscures not only the degree to which Native nations enjoyed repeated military success over the United States, but, in Burns's reproductions, also the powerful recent and continuing impact of Native nationalism.[63]

Jay Cooke hoped that by imposing abstract delimitations on a section of "scenic" western space, by inventing a park, he could help reverse the devaluation of his overbuilt rail system. Yet, in order to realize the gain of receipts from passenger travel to the western public reserve, another sort of reserve would also have to be created, or, as it were, adjusted. These "reserves," concentrations of the victims of capital, not capital itself, contained the hostile Sioux, Crow, Blackfeet, and other nations with which the United States was at war in the West.[64] Thus, in 1873 a commission was formed to negotiate even more territory from the Crow, who had already surrendered a great deal by the Fort Laramie Treaty of 1868. According to Edward P. Smith, the commissioner of Indian affairs:

> Such an extent of territory being greatly in excess of the quantity required for the necessities of the Indians, and the northern boundary thereof throughout its entire length, being in close proximity to the

proposed line of the Northern Pacific Railroad, it is desirable that the
Indians should relinquish to the Government at least a portion thereof,
and consent to confine themselves within more circumscribed limits. It
is with this end primarily in view that you should conduct your negotiations under the foregoing appointment.[65]

The revised territory could be considered excessive only if the Crow were both
reduced in numbers and lived as farmers instead of hunters. The interests of Jay
Cooke's road were intended both to invent a national park and to transform radically (or exterminate) a hostile culture. The intentions of the 1873 commission, to
secure territory for the railroad that actively instigated the formation of Yellowstone Park, represent the clear evidence of the production of capitalist space and
the invention of nationalist place. The creation of the park would, among other
things, produce a fantastic "safe space" in the midst of the West which, though
remarkably untrue in 1872, the military would eventually "realize" through years
of warfare. The park was created in contested territory, but did much to facilitate
the transformation of the West from a space characterized by imperialist violence
to a space of consumption (tourism) and production (wealth).

Yellowstone National Park was established by an act of Congress in 1872, four
years *before* Custer and his troops were killed by a strong, and yet much depleted,
coalition of Native forces about 120 miles to the *east* of the park's northeast
border. For the first years of its history Yellowstone functioned not primarily as a
recreational or scenic park, but as a military outpost during war. Thus, in 1875,
three years after Yellowstone was founded, General William Terry, seeing that
simmering hostilities were once again heading for all-out war with the Sioux,
commissioned Captain William Ludlow, another topographical engineer, to map
areas of the park and determine logistical details—including appropriate sites for
new forts.[66] A year earlier, in July and August of 1874, Ludlow had accompanied,
as topographical expert, Colonel George Custer into the Black Hills to map and
gather military information. Civilian prospectors were included on this expedition,
which suggests that the expedition was less about *preparing* for war, as General
Sheridan proposed, than about precipitating war for the seizure of the Black
Hills—an area which was unambiguously a part of Sioux territory according to the
Fort Laramie treaty of 1868.[67]

The events that led to the Sioux War of 1876 are familiar and offer themselves
to interpretation according to the frame I have provided. Between 1870-72 the
Northern Pacific Railroad expanded quickly across the Dakota prairie to the
Missouri River while surveyors worked ahead into the Yellowstone Valley, much
to the chagrin of the Sioux and Crow. Robert Utley notes that "[w]hether the
projected route of the Northern Pacific up the Yellowstone Valley violated Sioux

territory as described by the treaty of 1868 might have been debated at some length—although, strangely, it was not."[68] The capitalist production of space was not to be challenged. The Panic of 1873 halted work on the railroad. In fact, economic historians have concluded that the financial collapse of the Northern Pacific was the precipitating factor for the Panic.[69] When the abstract profits of ticket sales and speculative development were no longer viable, interest turned immediately to the mining of gold and the "reserved" space of Indian territory was invaded: "By the winter of 1875-76, the President and the Interior Department were winking at about 15,000 miners in the Black Hills."[70] The larger social/ideological function of this kind of "frontier" space (one where wealth was imagined as so immediately extractable) is to elaborate the myth of opportunity to the urban proletariat being squeezed by economic depression. In the hopes of promoters like Cooke and other industrialists, it helps stop revolutions and enhances the value of both urban and western space, as Richard Slotkin notes: "The credible promise that present labor would make possible future 'success' constituted an ideological safety valve for class discontent. The . . . Frontier was one metaphor for this promise, and it had some appeal for the working classes."[71]

Slotkin is correct to imply that the appeal of the "frontier" for the working class may have been limited, but this points more than anything to the ideological origins of frontier promotions.[72] The safety-valve idea was, after all, an ideological invention, and the fact that it may have been ignored suggests the resistance of workers to ideological deployments. The popular press clearly associated the opening of western land with the defusion of class conflict. The *New York World* referred to the prospectors anxious to exploit the Black Hills as "A Tide that Cannot be Stopped," and continued that "disappointed and impoverished gold hunters . . . make pretty good farmers, and the soil of the Black Hills is said to be rich."[73]

Indeed, the 1870s saw the development of open class war in America that clamored, to hegemonic interests, for ideological and often violent containment. And it was precisely the railroads, Jay Cooke's in particular, that precipitated this radically unstable social situation; and so it was along the railroad network that the most violent strikes broke out: "It was the railroad corporations whose operations had produced the largest urban concentrations of proletariat; and railroads whose importation of labor from Ireland and China had given to the new working class a 'foreign' character; and it was in the railroad yards that the fiery labor uprising of 1877 would begin."[74] Slotkin has best outlined, in economic and ideological terms, the role that the "frontier" played in the multifaceted social transformations during the immediate post-Reconstruction era.

According to Slotkin, the Civil War was, on one level, fought for the small farmer and artisan as part of a continuing effort to realize the Jeffersonian and Jacksonian promise of America. In this regard, the aristocratic Southern monopoly on land was to be opened to freedmen (forty acres and a mule), and, of course, free and independent labor for all people was a crucial aspect of the Northern rhetoric. Nevertheless, Slotkin notes, "the new order the war created was one in which the 'producer' [by which he means worker and artisan] and his economic self-sufficiency were no longer the primary political and economic values. . . . [T]he ideological shift after the war was rooted in a rejection of this premise, in favor of a counter-assertion."[75] This counter-assertion prioritized the rights of capital according to the notion that, in an advanced industrial state (that the Civil War decidedly helped America to become), "where the scale of enterprise requires huge drafts of capital and the mustering of masses of labor, it is capital that creates the basis for production, capital that is the generator of national wealth."[76]

In such a situation, where the "frontier myth" (according to Slotkin, an elaborate set of often explicitly violent and always aggressive symbols, images, and rhetorics promising the opportunity for wealth for all people) was economically under hard critique, the transformation and elaboration of the myth became ideologically crucial for an economic system that relied on capital expansion and its necessary correlate, western migration, to relieve crisis. However, because by the 1870s the corporation had superceded the individual as the privileged agent of national progress, the "rituals of war and sacrifice associated with the Frontier conquest would be undertaken not in the name of the family but in that of the railroad."[77] At the same time, the rhetorical principle of economic independence would hardly be jettisoned—it would be asserted with more vigor in an effort to "paper over" the ruling interests. Jay Cooke reveals the overdetermination of Slotkin's "frontier" metaphor by the fact that he advanced his subsidized (land grant) railroad by propagandizing a "garden in the West," at once revealing and obscuring the terms and economics of expansion. Rhetorically, the "garden" was the resource for *independence and wealth* that laborers, like those building the railroad, would soon be able to realize. The "garden myth" thus held the essential promise of the "frontier" according to Slotkin, but at the same time it obscured the violent contest, both actual and imagined, appurtenant to expansion.

Cooke invented a propaganda pamphlet for recruiting immigrants and investors for the land grant region and railroad, respectively. To the immigrant Cooke promised civilization and progress: "The belt of the country tributary to the Northern Pacific Road is within the parallels of latitude which in Europe, Asia, and America embrace the most enlightened, creative, and progressive populations."[78] In the vein of Jeffersonian environmentalism, the climate and resources were naturally bound to constitute a nationally, if not globally powerful population. In his huge land grant, which, Cooke asserted, held the room for "ten states as large as Massachusetts," the prospective immigrant would find "a soil, a climate, and resources of coal, timber, ores of metal, and perpetual waterpower, altogether superior to those upon which Massachusetts has become populous, rich, refined and politically powerful."[79] An idealization of the immigrant Irish experience was used as a model for the gross promise of Cooke's great country, or colony—a model to be exceeded.

The region was advertised as so rich and fertile that its *not* becoming the most powerful region of the country was apparently next to impossible. The weather metonymically promised the best of all worlds:

> The subject of the temperature of the belt with which lies the Land Grant of the Northern Pacific Railroad, cannot be better summed up than by repeating that Minnesota has the average temperature of North-ern New York without its discomfort and chill; Dakota, that of Iowa, with a drier and more invigorating air; Montana, that of Ohio without its dampness and changeableness. . . . The South-west winds, carry the rain-clouds eastward over the continental divide, and distribute their moisture over the Fertile Belt stretching from the mountains to the lakes.[80]

Of the Yellowstone Valley in particular the pamphlet asserts that "some of the other valleys are beautiful. This is grand. It abounds in magnificent scenery, most excellent farm-sites, and water-powers. . . . The surrounding mountains are full of gold and silver-bearing quartz. . . . Forty bushels [of wheat] an acre is not an unusual crop in the Yellowstone Valley."[81] Unsurprisingly, the region bore the publicity title of "Cooke's Banana Belt."

As the immigrant was sure to become a wealthy and powerful element of American culture—a constituted American—the investor was likewise sure to become rich. While claiming that rail volume would exceed any other transconti-nental road, Cooke refers to the earnings of the Central Pacific to forecast returns: "The Central Pacific Railroad has earned, in six years, more than $10,000,000 *net* over operating expenses, and nearly $6,000,000 *over operating expenses and interest on its Bonds*; while, during *four and a half* of that time, the Road was under construction, without through business, and, for the first three years, with less than 100 miles in operation."[82] The profits from the Northern Pacific, accord-ing to Cooke, could only be greater.

Cooke was trying to produce space and to make space produce a profit. He needed immigrants for the traffic of passengers and freight, and, despite having already invested over five million dollars of his personal capital, he needed more money to build the "profitable" road. He filed another chapter in the myth of the garden to produce his capitalist space. His capacity to distribute the myth was enormous. Journalists and cultural figures like Horace Greeley and Henry Ward Beecher invested in the irresistible promise of plenty and profit ($20,000 and $15,000 respectively) then used their influence to bring others aboard.[83]

In various ways Cooke's invention of the upper plains as a garden of power and profit could not withstand reality. The growing season was short, the winters brutal, and the rainfall meager. Yet, one Cooke "garden" has withstood; in fact, it facilitated not only the production of space, but has become a central icon of American identity, a national symbolic place: Yellowstone National Park.

The terms by which contested western territory in and around Yellowstone was described in military reports, like those of the Langford expedition, reveal the inseparability of capital and government interests in inventing the American West through propaganda. Such reports did much to fit this space to an image in keeping with idealizations of the American landscape. I mean to suggest that the "frontier," as a site of capital investment and Indian war, was deliberately elaborated rhetorically as already within the union through the sheer familiarity of the "garden" landscape invoked. It is no small matter that a very similar landscape had, by 1873, already been constructed in the heart of New York City. From such a landscape any evidence of imperialism or violence is necessarily absent, however contrary to the actual history unfolding in the represented space, either frontier or urban. For the crucial point is that space is not so much being represented as it is representative of hegemonic interests that rely on the obfuscation of actual conflicts.

The military reports from various Yellowstone expeditions reiterated the rhetoric of peace and plenty fundamental to the propaganda directly elaborated to the worker, immigrant, tourist, and investor. For instance, Ludlow's 1875 report, like those to the region both before and after him is, unsurprisingly, mostly rather dry informative prose: "Wagons can be taken as far as the [Mammoth Hot] springs without much difficulty. . . . At the springs, however, wheels must be abandoned and everything carried upon pack animals."[84] The presence of this sort of language made the idealizations all the more palpable, as the military reports were not expected to be forums for either the picturesque or the Tall Tale. Captain Raynolds, writing of his 1860 expedition drafted the following description of Yellowstone Valley: "Through the valley, in the centre, the stream could be seen placidly winding its way, a subduing element in the grandeur of a scene whose glories pen cannot adequately describe and only the brush of a Bierstadt or a Stanley could portray on canvas."[85] Captain Barlow wrote of the same valley after his 1871 expedition: "In that direction is a valley almost level, slightly rising toward the mountains on either side, with a beautiful, clear stream winding through the center, whose current was so gentle that its direction could not, as yet, be determined. Grass and flowers covered the hill-side, interspersed with occasional groves of balsam, ceder and spruce."[86]

Barlow's myth making is revealed by his odd mixture of tenses as he slips from the declarative to the indeterminate. However peaceful these various (yet similar) renderings of the landscape, the formation of Yellowstone Park, to which these reports contributed (both Barlow and Ludlow actively supported the park idea after it was initiated by Langford), was not intended to preserve "wilderness" from the encroachments of commerce, but rather to empty through war the "wild" of its bite so that commerce could thrive.[87] This is revealed, ironically, through the confluence of tourism and violence.

In the summer of 1877, one year after Custer's defeat, five years after the Park was founded and in the midst of the worst year of class violence in American history, members of two groups of tourists visiting the park were killed or wounded, and the U.S. military was put on its heels, by the Nez Perces. According to an 1855 treaty the Nez Perces ceded much of their territory to the United States, but when, in 1860, gold was discovered by miners on their reservation prospectors moved into Nez Perces territory and built the permanent town of Lewiston, in violation of the standing treaty. In 1863 the United States "invented" a new treaty, which went unrecognized and unsigned by the nation's leaders, including Chief Joseph.

It was at this time that what historian Gregory Evans Dowd terms a "spirited resistance" was rising among the Nez Perces.[88] The following is a nearly contemporaneous description by Hiram Chittenden, the historian and avid promoter of Yellowstone Park:

> [The Nez Perces] fell under the influence of a class of mystics called "dreamers," who taught a doctrine of land ownership which was the immediate cause of all their subsequent troubles. This doctrine was, in substance, that the "Creative Power," when He made the earth, made no marks, no lines of division or separation, upon it, and that it should be allowed to remain as it is; that it "should not be disturbed by man, and that any cultivation of the soil, or other improvements, and voluntary submission to the control of government, 'were incompatible with the true purpose for which it was made.'" At bottom it was the broad principle that no man or aggregation of men can take from other men the right to enjoy what nature has made for all.[89]

One thing Chittenden does is draw a remarkably explicit equation between the

Nez Perces and masses of American laborers by suggesting that the more-or-less harmless Indians had fallen under the influence of "outside" agitators who preach a "socialist" philosophy, and that such an influence was responsible for their destruction.[90] Otherwise, we may presume, they would have remained happy with their lot. As Chittenden goes on to comment, the United States had no choice but to enforce the terms of the "treaty" and precipitate hostilities. The final sentence contains the staggering irony of the passage, as it uses precisely the rhetoric deployed to justify the creation of the National Park: a space reserved for the enjoyment of all people, forever outside the dangers of "private" ownership. Thus, the 1872 Act of Dedication for Yellowstone National Park: "[The area] is hereby reserved and withdrawn from settlement, occupancy, or sale under the laws of the United States, and dedicated and set apart as a public park or pleasuring ground for the benefit and enjoyment of the people."[91] The Indians are removed by force and a park is invented in the space where their history, and the history of imperialist violence, has been performed only to be violently erased.[92] Here Catlin's fantasy of a minuscule Indian presence is exceeded. Ostensibly harboring a "dangerous" philosophy of public ownership the Indians are killed or interned in a violent act of geographic dispossession—on land set aside "for everyone."

It is a potent irony of Yellowstone National Park that it was legally founded as a space "outside" the "perils" of private ownership by means of violent dispossession; further, that those from whom the land was being appropriated were regarded as barbaric or subhuman in large part because they did recognize the principle of private property. The irony deepens when it is revealed that a rhetorical equation is drawn between the Indians and the "foreign" (or foreign influenced) workers squeezed to the point of rupture by an economic depression precipitated by railroad expansion toward Yellowstone, financed by the propaganda of "valuable" space. The Yellowstone region was deeply involved in the dynamics of two red scares, and it was explicitly intended to deal with both (this is not to say it succeeded). An understood point of equation between the "barbaric denizen" of the urban "wilderness" that so troubled Olmsted and other urban reformers, and the "barbaric" Indian is disclosed: they both have some stiff objections to the hegemonic control of property. Relatedly, both the worker and the Indian represent powerful forces unambiguously capable of militaristically challenging the social order that thrives on the monopolistic control of territory and capital.

3.

Five years after the Nez Perces incident, visiting tourists were still anxious about the potential of Indian attacks. Mary Bradshaw Richards, in a series of travel letters written in 1882 to the *Salem Observer*, assures herself that her "camp is close to a battleground where the Nez Perces were defeated" (in fact, the Nez Perces were not defeated in the park), but continues her account anxiously:

> As darkness came on we reclined on the grass and were listening to a story about a "good Indian" when we spied far back on the prairie a horseman coming rapidly toward us. We were sixty-five miles from human habitations, we four alone, with only the courage of three men, one shotgun and a pair of revolvers for defense. I listened for a war-whoop, almost expecting to see a whole band of savages appear at the heels of the rider. Who, save an Indian, and a very bad one too, could ride like the coming guest?[93]

A "good Indian," we should need little reminder, is a dead Indian. The rider, it turns out, was a park employee.

The rhetoric of democratic experience that justified the park, the idea that it was for the benefit of "everyone," obscures the fact that it was only the relatively wealthy who could afford to visit Yellowstone. Richards describes the accouterments of the tourists on a two-week tour of the park:

> Our outfit (two persons), consisted of a wall tent, blankets, buffalo skins, axe, hatchet, nails, ropes, hammer and wheel grease; flour, sugar, lard, ham, eggs packed in oats, canned meats, fruits, jellies; a long tailed frying pan, bake kettle, coffee pot, tin plated cups and spoons, knives and forks; a capital driver, an accomplished cook, two large balky horses and lastly the all important spring wagon. . . . This outfit cost us eighteen dollars per day.[94]

Yellowstone National Park functioned as a "purified" space, ideally emptied of Indians and violence. By means of its spatial construction, it established rhetorically the "openness" of the West crucial to capitalist development, that is, the consumption of capital overaccumulation in, primarily, the form of railroad development. The spatial rhetoric of Yellowstone is a more profound material force than verbal rhetoric because it is always a component of the built environment: it is a construction which facilitates more profitable constructions. Such spatial rhetoric was thus an important force in the resolution of the nineteenth century's most threatening crisis. It was, I conclude, a prime instrument in the redemption of America, a status it shared with the urban park.

New York's Central Park, like Yellowstone Park, was a space related to imperialist violence. In a city rife with class antagonisms, the urban park presented a fantasy where the western landscape—crowded in actuality with Native nations and a war in which the success of the United States was by no means guaranteed—was reconstructed as a spectacular panorama emptied of all signs of imperialist processes, including both people and war. Thus it was several years after Central Park was opened before Park patrons were allowed off the walks and roads. The presence of actual bodies in the idealized landscape threatened too dearly fantasy with reality. The Park was designed as a representational space, in which, as Henri Lefebvre writes, we are sure to find "exquisite lines, refined pleasures, the sumptuous and cruel dissipation of wealth accumulated by any and every means."[95] The Park was, and remains, a representation of power, where capital accumulation is abstracted into the space of the *picturesque*: "To expand our finite faculties and afford them a culture both profound and elevating, Nature is spread around us, with all its stupendous proportions, and Revelations speaks to us of an eternal augmentation of knowledge hereafter, for weal or woe."[96] The Park is also an ideological institution organizing public experience and the movements of bodies through space in facilitation of commerce and consumption.

Not only was the urban park founded amid the violence of the Indian wars and urban class conflict, but urban parks were, and remain, as we all know, a dangerous place to be after dark. Writing in "Greensward" of the roads for communication and commerce that would traverse Central Park, Olmsted states, they "will also have to be kept open, while the park proper will be useless for any good purpose after dusk; for experience has shown that even in London, with its admirable police arrangements, the public cannot be secured safe transit through large open spaces of ground after nightfall" (*PFLO* V: 121). The main roads across Central Park are sunk below the level of the park both to keep the sight of commerce hidden from Park patrons during the day (thus further obscuring the park's "central" function) and to keep those same patrons safe from the "dangerous classes" that "take over" the park in the dark. Central Park was provided with its own police force both to regulate how it was to be used and to control the inevitable violence of such a "democratic" space.

Despite widespread interest, imperialism remains a rather undertheorized and underdescribed phenomenon in the context of nineteenth-century urban America. The national park and the urban park were important parts of the functional fantasy of American imperialism. In the West a bounded space was "preserved," ostensibly to provide the American public with the natural resources necessary for its physical and moral *redemption*. Olmsted, as part of his preliminary report on the benefits of "setting aside" the Yosemite region as a park (also quoted in chapter two) wrote that,

It is a scientific fact that the occasional contemplation of natural scenes of an impressive character . . . is favorable to the health and vigor of men and especially to the health and vigor of their intellect beyond any other conditions which can be offered them, that it not only gives pleasure for the time being but increases the subsequent capacity for happiness and the means for securing happiness. (*PFLO* V: 502)

Those are the same notions used to justify Yellowstone's founding. It was in large part because it was understood that commerce took its toll on the mental and physical health of individuals that the national park, and later parks, were created. But redemption is more than just a matter of self-empowerment. When the experience, or transformation, involves an entire culture, or at least a large segment of a culture, it expresses itself largely through patterns of movement—massive migrations through a particular space—not to mention particular transformations of spatial arrangements. When Olmsted rallied for the securing of Niagara Falls as a public park, he was explicitly seeking to "redeem" America in the eyes of the world. A symbolic national monument had been lost to hucksters and con artists, claimed Olmsted, and he wrote about the need for preserving such natural monuments to prove to the world that there was civilization in America.[97] Yet we must not forget that redemption is intended to bring spiritual prosperity, and, what is more, as the term suggests, financial returns.

The notion of "redemption" has a particular inflection in the nineteenth century. During the panics of 1857 and 1873, banks across the United States suspended specie payments either entirely or in part. In lieu of specie payments, bank notes were issued that did much to increase the financial havoc. The notes were issued as change for as little as a penny. As bank failure and note forgery was rampant, the authority of such script was abysmally low. With no gold to back the notes, *redemption* was often impossible to come by.[98] America's parks were the objects of venture capital as if Nature were secure script, or a "winning ticket," at least such was the hope of Jay Cooke and the Northern Pacific Railroad.

In the abstract space of the capitalist environment, a space in which the real manifestations of crisis unfold, where capital both threatens itself and thrives on its own contradictions, the complex ideological dynamics of consumption always stand behind the facades of buildings and trees. It is the permanent and terrible evidence of the relentless accumulation of capital. Overaccumulation manifests an overabundance—whether of banks, parks, goods, or workers—as capital fights itself, and, as history has so far demonstrated, prospers. Crisis and redemption: one description of the dialectic of capitalist history. Redemption thus requires consumption—as consumption is crucial for any passage through a crisis of overaccumulation—and the space of Nature is elaborated, in the nineteenth cen-

tury, to facilitate the prosperity evidenced by the geographic expansion of capitalism. In the urban park, America's imperialist fantasy, its imaginary space of an
endless land of goods and resources, is reconstructed to do the hard ideological
work of containing class violence through its consumption of workers and capital.
If a crucial objective for the planners of capitalist development is figuring a way
to maintain the value of the old built environment while at the same time opening
up and exploring a fresh space for accumulation, then America's first parks, both
urban and "wilderness," must stand as profound monuments of the effort exerted
toward this objective.

Conclusion

Not only Hegel's hope that reason would shape and control reality, but Marx's hope that reason would be embodied in a revolutionary class and rational socialist society, had come to naught.

> —Douglas Kellner, introduction to Marcuse's *One Dimensional Man*

Strictly speaking nature is not some particular thing we can point to, and it has no opposite.

> —Gina Crandell, *Nature Pictorialized*

I remain ambivalent about what should probably be regarded by sociologists and demographers (among whom I do not number) as one of the great tragedies of modern record keeping: the loss of Frederick Law Olmsted's meticulous statistical "investigation" of thousands of Union recruits that he compiled as head of the Sanitary Commission during the Civil War. What did Olmsted intend to do with this information? Help win the war is only part of the answer; Olmsted gathered the information as evidence of the dearth of hygenic discipline among immigrants, the rural poor, and the working class. Olmsted found the recruits "really much dirtier than it can be believed they have been accustomed to in their civil life" (*PFLO* IV: 12). Olmsted hoped to keep the "dirt" of barbarism out of the nation: "If five hundred thousand of our young men could be made to acquire something of the characteristic habits of soldiers in respect to the care of their habitations, their persons, and their clothing, by the training of this war, the good that they would afterwards do as unconscious missionaries of a healthful reform throughout the country, would be by no means valueless to the nation" (*PFLO* IV: 12). Indeed. The war was, for Olmsted, another opportunity for reformism. One can imagine the wounded soldiers' response to the Sanitary Commission agents and their program of discipline and hygiene—being told to clean up their act as they sat, suffered, and died. Walt Whitman, who worked so steadily to relieve the suffering of soldiers, attests: "As to the Sanitary commission & the like, I am sick of them all . . . you ought to see the way the men as they lie helpless in bed turn their faces from the sight of these Agents, Chaplains, &c . . . they seem to me always a set of foxes & wolves."[1] I find it compelling, the idea of Olmsted as the chief officer of predators feeding on the "lower orders" with whom his own relationship was so ambivalent.

On January 5, 1997, art reporter Richard B. Woodward covered an exhibition titled "Viewing Olmsted" for the *New York Times*. Introducing his report on the photographic celebration of Frederick Law Olmsted's legacy, Woodward wrote the following: "Has the work of any 19th century American artist worn as well as the parks of Frederick Law Olmsted? More revered, cared for and needed now than at any time since he and his partners first drew them, his rough-hewn green spaces constitute perhaps the finest public art ever created in North America. Oases that increasingly sustain the cities that have engulfed them, his landscapes are for millions of people the sole trace of wilderness left in daily life."[2]

Woodward's extraordinary praise for Olmsted is based on a rather anxious concern for individual and municipal survival, as demonstrated by his endorsement of another reporter, from whom he quotes: if "New Yorkers all woke up tomorrow and found that Central Park had become 150 blocks of high-rise housing, then a week from tomorrow there would be no New York City." By this account, to suggest that Central Park is more "needed now than at any time since" its invention is to generously understate the park's value. Yet, caught up in a kind of cata-strophic fantasizing, Woodward neglects to elaborate why, in the late 1990s, Olmsted's park is so needed, and his only suggestion of what the park so crucially offers is rather vague: "wilderness." Wilderness would appear to relieve potentially devastating tension in the city and its inhabitants—it "sustains" them. As ecologists have recently announced the world's rain forests the "lungs" of the planet, so Central Park would appear to be the vital organ of New York City; without it, the city dies.

It is not surprising that a natural space is articulated according to a biological metaphor, one that facilitates the anthropomorphizing of the city according to its inhabitants and their understood need for green space. Yet such metaphors and projections, which constitute the city as an organic entity maintained by a natural vital organ, function to obscure what Woodward seems always on the point of revealing, that Olmsted's "green space" maintains not only a local but also a national, and even global, economy: hence his hyperbolic praise and his reference to "North America."

The vital economic function of green space is more clearly revealed in another section of the same issue of the *Times*, where there appears a report by Anthony DePalma headlined "Popularity Brings a Huge Canadian Park to Crisis." DePalma covers Alberta's Banff National Park and the various angles surrounding an October 1996 report by independent scientists who concluded that "there is a crisis at Banff so severe that unless something is done soon, it will cease to be a park."[3] It is precisely economic development that threatens Banff: "With three major ski areas . . . 5,600 hotel rooms, 1,300 businesses, the Canadian Pacific Railway, the four-lane Trans-Canada Highway, 27 holes of golf and over five million visitors a year [the park] is more popular than ever. And more endangered." The more anecdotal evidence of threatening development includes the presence of a new Hard Rock Café and a Ralph Lauren shop just down the street from a restaurant that serves buffalo fondue.

If, as the report on Olmsted would have it, in New York nature averts crisis by sustaining the city, in Banff the city precipitates crisis by developing over "nature." In Banff's backcountry trails are eroding, native fish are being displaced by stocked trout, cars and trucks are killing too many elk and bear, and urban sprawl is "artificially dividing the herds of animals, raising the problem of inbreeding." The crisis in Banff is one of borders. The space of "nature" and the space of the city are not adequately marked and maintained by strict delimitation. I would suggest that a reason for this is precisely because the Banff park was intended to serve primarily an economic function. As the *Times* reporter duly notes, "railroaders pushed the [Canadian] government to declare the [Banff] hot springs a national park." The railroaders sought tourist revenue and built the massive Banff Springs Hotel themselves to help assure the realization of profit. The cities that now crowd and "contaminate" the park indicate the economic success of the park's creation; at this foundational level, the current "crisis" indicates the Banff Park has more than achieved the goals its promoters sought, namely, the production of value and profit from a "natural" and, in capitalist terms, previously unincorporated space. We continue to struggle with the legacy of the deployments of "nature."

In America, urban and national parks were first created in the latter half of the nineteenth century. As I have submitted, they were related essentially not so much as preserves of "nature"—which was their rhetorical justification—but as instruments deployed to control contested space, constitute a stable class and national identity, and to assure the reproduction of the dominant social order during times of profound crises, when capital overaccumulation precipitated major economic depressions that led to widespread worker radicalization and class conflict, in turn profoundly threatening national (capitalist) unity. America's first parks were at

I find this hard to believe still

once, to some degree, produced by and productive of the panics which occurred so
near their respective founding moments. Produced amid crises, the parks were also
created to preempt class warfare and obscure class difference—the most serious
threats to the reproduction of the capitalist social order in the later nineteenth
century. Additionally, they were created to help maintain or to produce the exchange value of a particular space, frontier or urban, and, inseparably, to maintain
and fortify the class differences they worked to obscure. That is, they were productive and consumptive spaces directly in the service of expanding (even if crisis
prone) capitalism.

again, I see the "obscure" part - the fortify part mostly comes in the founding

As I explained in chapter one, class struggle or militant organization in urban
centers devalues, in capitalist terms, such centers. When workers become strongly
organized, demand higher wages or better conditions, an entire built environment
of production and consumption may be abandoned. Enormous capital investments
are left to rust as mobile capital departs for some arena where lower wages can be
secured. Though cities may annex territory, they are, decidedly, immobile. For an
urban center to devalue also, and relatedly, means it becomes less efficient and
effective at reproducing the social order it is constructed to serve. The concept of
reproduction, is, of course, itself a "natural," or biological metaphor for social
processes by which human beings, with potential agency, are socialized and
controlled, or governed, such that they act or work in their own interest only to the
degree that such an interest is also an interest of the social order. This is hardly to
say that people do not, or cannot, act contrary to such socially profitable ways. It
is only to say that there is an infinite number of powerful devices intended to assure
that they do not. In urban space, the park was one such device within, but not
subordinate to, the greater socially reproductive concept of Nature. The urban park
was to resist the devaluing of urban space by defusing class conflict through the
consumption of excess labor and capital, through the elaboration of a visual and
spatial rhetoric intended to cultivate an ideal, nationalist identity, or, constitute
"citizens," and, relatedly, by working to both secure and obscure class differences.

Throughout this volume I have been concerned to describe how class is
obscured. I want, briefly, and finally, to emphasize my thesis: class obfuscation
functions to assure that class difference persists. Class difference, after all, does
persist; without it capitalism does not survive, let alone prosper, and all the
evidence—including the enormous exploitation of people and natural resources—suggests that capitalism has prospered. Because of my critique of institutions many in the American green movement consider cherished and hard won I
have had, at nearly every stage of the development of my research, to answer to the
charge of antienvironmentalism. That my point could be so often so far missed has
been exasperating. That capitalist prosperity is realized by the simultaneous

finally

exploitation of people and natural resources should be obvious; it is not obvious because "nature" has been deployed to confuse us about the form and the terms of exploitation. *(who is missing what point exactly?) (here he drops the pt.)*

Lefebvre writes: "Capitalism has found itself able to attenuate (if not resolve) its internal contradictions. . . . We cannot calculate at what price, but we do know the means: by occupying space, by producing a space."[4] While Lefebvre's insight (one would hope his influence) is extraordinary, as Neil Smith notes, his "rethinking of nature is poor."[5] It is certainly my hope that this book has contributed to a rethinking of "nature" in the context of theorizing and describing the relation of space to capitalism. I would like to conclude by rendering my theorization more explicit. I want, in particular, to connect the ideas I have developed in this volume with the thorny "problem" of ideology. By this "problem" I do not mean the tremendous difficulty of overcoming the multitudinous forms of ideological deployments; I mean the problem of understanding and explaining the existence of ideology itself.

I want to begin with a general proposition: "Democracy" requires the consent of "the people" to maintain authority. Yet social interests are at least as diverse as the class divisions of any given society. Etienne Balibar grapples with the complex and contradictory means by which "the people" are at once compelled and condemned to preserve a social and economic order that is not in their majority interest. According to Balibar, who is, albeit, considering the French Revolutionary period and texts, a nation founded on an "*absolute* notion of national sovereignty [has effectively introduced] a mimetic inversion of the monarchial sovereignty that it opposed in order to legitimate the representation of the people."[6] Instead of a "one and indivisible" monarchial will, a "general will" is put into service, "equally one and indivisible, equally the depository of all authority, but founded in the last analysis only upon the individuals who make up the nation."[7] Thus, in the words of the U.S. Constitution, "We the People" rhetorically strains to assume continuity of authority at a moment of radical political disruption. The phrase, backed by the presumably unanimous principles that the "Declaration of Independence" expounds, represents the paradoxical manner by which individuals assume a collective identity, or, the means by which the social duties of citizenship replace the natural rights of the individual that stood as the prime philosophical foundation of revolution in the first place.

A fundamental contradiction has been introduced which will be a more-or-less constant source of conflict and confrontation, as two classes have been brought into alliance by what Balibar calls a concept of "egalitarian sovereignty," which is, "practically a contradiction in terms, but the only way radically to expel all transcendence and to inscribe the political and social order in the element of immanence, of the auto-constitution of the people."[8] Thus,

> the Revolution, from the beginning, is not, is already no longer, a "bourgeois revolution," but a revolution made jointly by the bourgeoisie and the people and the nonbourgeois masses, in an ongoing relation of alliance and confrontation. The revolution is immediately grappling with its own internal contestation, without which it would not even exist, and always chasing after the unity of its opposites.[9]

How is service to a transcendent order preserved in such a fundamentally conflicted social and political situation? In large part it is preserved by nationalism and ideology. Of course, ideology, or the misrecognition of real social and political relations, is a paradoxical concept, arising as it does "out of a derivation of the 'superstructure'. . . from the 'base' constituted by 'real life,' by production."[10] If elements of the superstructure are derived from the base, then how is it that a form of consciousness occurs that is defined by the very inability to correctly perceive the character of the base? Balibar writes: "[Ideology] could essentially be said to be a theory of social consciousness . . . and the point would be to understand how that consciousness could both remain dependent on social being . . . while gaining increasing autonomy from it, to the point where it caused an unreal, fantastic 'world' to emerge . . . which substituted itself for real history."[11]

In fact, at particular points in history, especially during times of national and/or economic depression and crisis, "real history" is so utterly apparent that the "substitution" must be effected by the agency of *intellectuals* (broadly conceived as a kind of subclass both within and adjacent to the dominant class)—often in combination with sheer violence. On the role of intellectuals Balibar cites Hegel, who, in *The Philosophy of Right*, explains that in the modern state intellectuals are essential functionaries who discover their "true destiny" in the state. In Balibar's words, the "State which is universal for Hegel 'in itself' 'frees' the intellectuals (from belief and the various forms of personal dependence), so that they may be in its service, within the whole of society, perform an activity of mediation . . . and thus carry a universality which is as yet abstract to the level of 'self-consciousness.'"[12]

It is not that intellectuals are always consciously instrumentalist in their service to the dominant class, but that they have access to and prosper from the material resources by which they are, as a group, constituted, and thus they inevitably cultivate the persistence of the enabling conditions for their being. In other words, ideology as a form of consciousness is a historically manifested condition first and foremost of those formally divided from the conditions of production. Their misrecognition has, in turn, ideological effects, in so far as they command the cultural and technological resources that are manifested in the real world. Intellectuals—those who produce the dominant meanings, cultural, scientific or technological, by which people understand their world and act upon it—constitute the first order of ideology and their creations are ideological insofar as these bridge and reconstitute the intellectuals' actual alienated condition in the material world. The crucial role of the ideology of American exceptionalism is at once to obscure and perpetuate the fundamental class divisions of a capitalist society.

American first parks perpetuate the ideology of American exceptionalism through the material effect of spatial production and the nationalist process of the invention of place. When American capitalist prosperity was threatened—by the devaluations associated with financial crisis, the protests of workers, and Native contestations—parks were deployed.

Notes

Introduction: The Geography of Exceptionalism

1. Recent discussions of the "nature" of parks include Kenneth R. Olwig, "Reinventing Common Nature: Yosemite and Mount Rushmore—A Meandering Tale of a Double Nature," in *Uncommon Ground: Rethinking the Human Place in Nature,* ed. William Cronon (New York: W. W. Norton, 1996), 379-408; Neil Evernden, *The Social Creation of Nature* (Baltimore: Johns Hopkins University Press, 1992).

2. I state this at the outset to avoid confusion regarding vocabulary; this project is not explicitly intended as a contribution to the nature/culture debate, though some may find it useful as such. I will not be using the term "nature" to refer to that which is, presumably, not culture. Yet I will be discussing many people who do use "nature" in such a transparent manner. Whenever I am addressing the idea of nature as something, transparently, "out there," understood as noncultural, I will either use the term with a lowercase "n," or emphasize such a usage by placing the entire term in quotation marks. Whenever I am referring to what I consider an idealized concept or construction (as in parks) of the "natural," the term will appear with the first letter in uppercase. On the deepest level I feel that all uses of the term are, to some degree, idealized, but it will not be practical to fail to distinguish understood uses in what follows.

3. See David Sibley, *Geographies of Exclusion: Society and Difference in the West* (New York: Routledge, 1995). Sibley explains that "geographies of exclusion" are sociospatial boundaries where "power is expressed in the monopolization of space and the relegation of weaker groups in society to less desirable environments" (ix).

4. I have found Julia Kristeva's definition of "abjection" most useful for my work because she uses, while analyzing, the tropes commonly employed in the various discourses of the nineteenth-century period I am examining. Abjection, according to Kristeva, is a condition of the subject characterized by ambiguity where that against whom (or which) the subject defines himself (or, in the case of a state, itself) is never entirely absent from the subject. The "pure" subject is always, to some degree, "defiled." In the following I argue that Nature is a form of social and bodily regulation and repression of "pollution." See Julia Kristeva, *Powers of Horror: An Essay on Abjection* (New York: Columbia University Press,

1982). Sibley has also found Kristeva useful, see *Geographies*, 3-13.

5. See Raymond Williams, *Keywords: A Vocabulary of Society and Culture* (New York: Oxford University Press, 1976), 51-59.

6. Williams, *Keywords*, 52.

7. Henri Baudet, *Paradise on Earth: Some Thought on European Images of Non-European Man* (New Haven: Yale University Press, 1965), 55.

8. See Jack P. Greene, *The Intellectual Construction of America: Exceptionalism and Identity from 1492 to 1800* (Chapel Hill: University of North Carolina Press, 1993), 26.

9. For more on the Columbian era idea of America as a paradise see Greene, *Intellectual Construction*, 25-33; Durand Echeverria, *Mirage in the West: A History of the French Image of American Society to 1815* (Princeton: Princeton University Press, 1952); Loren Baritz, "The Idea of the West," *American Historical Review* 46 (1961): 617-40. This "utopian" exceptionalism is still an operative concept among some historians of the American West. For instance, David M. Wroble (*The End of American Exceptionalism: Frontier Anxiety from the Old West to the New Deal* [Lawrence: University Press of Kansas, 1993]) assumes a reiterated version of the Columbian rhetoric by equating the West with American uniqueness/possibility without interrogating the ideological function of such a construction. See also Martin Ridge, "Ray Allen Billington, Western History, and American Exceptionalism," *Pacific Historical Review* 56 (1987): 495-511.

10. Sir Thomas More, *Utopia*, in *The Complete Works of Sir Thomas More*, ed. Edward Surtz and J. H. Hexter, 4 vols. (New Haven: Yale University Press, 1965), 4: 49.

11. Greene, *Intellectual Construction*, 55.

12. Werner Sombart, *Why Is There No Socialism in the United States?* (New York: M. E. Sharpe, 1906). I have more to say about exceptionalism and the rise of anti-exceptionalism among labor historians in the following chapter.

13. Alexis de Tocqueville, *Democracy in America*, 2 vols. (New York: Vintage, 1990), 2: 36.

14. This, and all following Winthrop quotes are from John Winthrop, "A Modell of Christian Charity" (1630), in *Early American Writing*, ed. Giles Gunn (New York: Penguin, 1994), 108-09.

15. Hyman P. Minsky, "Financial Stability Revisited: The Economics of Disaster," in *Reappraisal of the Federal Reserve Discount Mechanism* (Washington, D.C.: U.S. Government Printing Office, 1972), 3: 95-136.

16. Charles P. Kindleberger, *Manias, Panics, and Crashes: A History of Financial Crises* (New York: Basic Books, 1978), 16.

17. Kindleberger, *Manias*, 17.

18. Kindleberger, *Manias*, 17.

19. See, for instance, the extensive references to Kindleberger throughout the following: Forrest Capie and Geoffrey E. Wood, eds., *Financial Crisis and the World Banking System* (New York: St. Martin's Press, 1986); Eugene N. White, ed., *Crashes and Panics: The Lessons from History* (Homewood, Ill.: Dow Jones, 1990).

20. Charles P. Kindleberger, "The Panic of 1873," in White, *Crashes*, 69-84.

21. See David Harvey, *Justice, Nature, and the Geography of Difference* (Cambridge, Mass.: Blackwell Publishers, 1996).

22. Because of Yellowstone's greater iconic status I discuss the meaning of "place" at greater length in chapter two, which focuses on Yellowstone. For now it should suffice to note that here, where I am referring to a "central" ideological arena, place refers to a richly symbolic and consciously elaborated visual and spatial rhetoric intended to constitute a general ideal and nationalist identity while at the same time preserving and elaborating the differences crucial to the capitalist division of labor.

23. The most culturally accurate definition of the sublime experience (that is, the definition most inscribed in the characteristic culturally constituted experience) is Edmund Burke's: "The passion caused by the great and sublime in nature . . . is astonishment, and astonishment is that state of the soul, in which all its motions are suspended, with some degree of horror. In this case the mind is so entirely filled with its object, that it cannot entertain any other, nor by consequence reason on that object which employs it" (Edmund Burke, *A Philosophical Inquiry into the Origin of Our Ideas of the Sublime and the Beautiful* [New York: Oxford University Press, 1990], 53). Kant's two-part theorization of the (mathematical and dynamic) sublime attempts to rescue reason from the experience Burke describes by exalting the rational subject capable of the infinite comprehension the sublime represents. This empowering of the subject is closer to what I will describe as the experience of the picturesque.

24. Elizabeth McKinsey, *Niagra Falls: Icon of the American Sublime* (Cambridge: Cambridge University Press, 1985), 251.

25. A thorough account of Native removal from the first national parks in Mark David Spence's recent book, *Dispossessing the Wilderness: Indian Removal and the Making of the National Parks* (New York: Oxford University Press, 1999). I draw upon and develop Spence's work in chapters two and four.

26. Lauren Berlant, *The Anatomy of National Fantasy: Hawthorne, Utopia, and Everyday Life* (Chicago: University of Chicago Press, 1992), 20.

Chapter One: Capital Contradictions

1. Walt Whitman, "Specimen Days" (May 16 to 22, 1879), in *Complete Prose Works* (Philadelphia: David McKay Publisher, 1897), 135.

2. Whitman, "Specimen Days," 134.

3. Whitman, "Specimen Days," 135.

4. Whitman, "Specimen Days," 135.

5. A recent story in the *New York Times* reviewing a celebratory presentation of and itself celebrating Olmsted's legacy correctly notes that "to a large extent, Frederick Law Olmsted laid the basis for the American landscape" (*New York Times*, 5 January 1997).

Extensive work has been done on the symbology of the picturesque landscape, yet the place of urban parks, particularly Central Park, in this history remains largely undeveloped. For the best history of Central Park see Roy Rozenzweig and Elizabeth Blackmar, *The Park and the People: A History of Central Park* (Ithaca: Cornell University Press, 1992). My debt to Rozenzweig and Blackmar will be plain in what follows; especially useful has been their discussion of Seneca Village (64-73). Other important works for understanding Olmsted's social context and personal "vision" include Albert Fein, ed., *Landscape into Cityscape: Frederick Law Olmsted's Plans for a Greater New York City* (Ithaca: Cornell University Press, 1968); David Schuyler, *The New Urban Landscape: The Redefinition of the City Form in Nineteenth-Century America* (Baltimore: Johns Hopkins University Press, 1986); Charles E. Beveridge, "Frederick Law Olmsted's Theory of Landscape Design," *Nineteenth Century* 3 (1977): 38-43; Thomas Bender, *Toward an Urban Vision: Ideas and Institutions in Nineteenth-Century America* (Lexington: University Press of Kentucky, 1975), 159-87. For the standard biography of Olmsted see Laura Wood Roper, *FLO: A Biography of Frederick Law Olmsted* (Baltimore: Johns Hopkins University Press, 1973). Olmsted has not gathered the quantity of ideological critique studies one might expect of such a crucial figure in the history of American public space; the best is certainly implicit within Rozenzweig and Blackmar's book. For a discussion of Olmsted's fundamental conservatism see Jeoffrey Blodgett, "Frederick Law Olmsted: Landscape Architecture As Conservative Reform," *Journal of American History* 62 (1976): 869-89.

Anne E. Mosher has written an extensive account of the efficacy of Olmsted's industrial town designs in suppressing labor organization. See her dissertation, "Capital Transformation and the Restructuring of Place: The Creation of a Model Industrial Town" (Pd.D. diss., Pennsylvania State University, 1989). Two other recent dissertations provide useful discussions of the political or ideological inflections of Olmsted's writing or designs. Elizabeth J. Donaldson places Olmsted in the history of American nature writing and suggests how he shared an ethic of material expansion characteristic of the era ("Picturesque Scenes, Sentimental Creatures: The Rhetoric and Politics of American Nature Writing, 1890-1920 " [Ph.D. diss., State University of New York at Stony Brook, 1997]). Kenneth Blair Hawkins discusses the connection between "theraputic" early nineteenth-centry asylum grounds and Olmsted's reformist designs ("The Therapeutic Landscape: Nature, Architecture, and Mind in Nineteenth-Century America" [Ph.D. diss., University of Rochester, 1991]).

6. Georg Wilhelm Friedrich Hegel, *The Philosophy of Right*, trans. T. M. Knox (New York: Dover, 1956), 150.

7. David Harvey, *The Urbanization of Capital* (Baltimore: Johns Hopkins University Press, 1985), 5-6.

8. Harvey, *Urbanization*, 5-6.

9. George Bataille, *The Accursed Share: An Essay on General Economy* (New York: Zone Books, 1988), 21.

10. Franklin Folsom, *Impatient Armies of the Poor: The Story of Collective Action of the Unemployed, 1808-1942* (Niwot, Colo.: University of Colorado Press, 1991), 84.

11. For instance, in the Lowell textile industries cheap female and child labor were at first employed, but when the women agitated for higher wages after the Civil War they were largely replaced by Irish immigrants. See Brian C. Mitchell, *The Paddy Camps: The Irish of Lowell, 1821-61* (Urbana: University of Illinois Press, 1988).

12. Hegel, *Philosophy of Right*, 150.

13. Hegel, *Philosophy of Right,* 150-51.

14. Georg Wilhelm Friedrich Hegel, *The Philosophy of History*, trans. J. Sibree (New York: Dover, 1956), 86.

15. Hegel, *Philosophy of History*, 87, my emphasis.

16. Slavog Zizek, *The Plague of Fantasies* (New York: Verso, 1997), 127.

17. In his meditation on the urban landscape in *The Country and the City*, Raymond Williams makes the point that the built environment of capitalism stands as a massive barrier to social change: "H. G. Wells once said, coming out of a political meeting where they had been discussing social change, that this great towering city was a measure of the obstacle, of how much must be moved if there was to be any change" (New York: Oxford University Press, 1973), 5.

18. Harvey, *Urbanization*, 71.

19. Patricia Hills, "Picturing Progress in the Era of Westward Expansion," in *The West as America: Reinterpreting Images of the Frontier, 1820-1920*, ed. William H. Truettner (Washington, D.C.: Smithsonian Institution Press, 1991), 100.

20. Much of the New Labor History of the 1970s and 80s can be fairly described as antiexceptionalist, elaborating the broad and radical class-conscious activity in nineteenth-century America that was similar to European movements. See Michael Shalev and Walter Korpi, "Working-Class Mobilization and American Exceptionalism," *Economic and Industrial Democracy* 1 (1980): 31-61; Wilentz, *Chants Democratic*; Byron E. Shafer, ed., *Is America Different? A New Look at American Exceptionalism* (Oxford: Clarendon Press, 1991).

In an exceptionalist vein I recognize the final failure of a radical working-class movement, a failure rightly located in early union racism and the general, similar failure to incorporate a nonskilled constituency. On early union racism see David R. Roediger, *The Wages of Whiteness: Race and the Making of the American Working Class* (London: Verso, 1991). On discrimination against the nonskilled see Ira Katzneson and Aristide Zolberg, eds., *Working-Class Formation* (Princeton: Princeton University Press, 1986).

I seek to contribute to an understanding of radicalism's failure through an analysis of how a hegemonically imposed construct, Nature, contributed to the manufacture of a nationalist identity that was necessarily racist and fragmenting to working-class solidarity. In an antiexceptionalist vein I recognize the power and influence working-class (and unemployed) movements represented during the major economic crises of the nineteenth century (that Nature helped to control). For more on the exceptionalist debate see Eric Foner, "Why Is There No Socialism in America?" *History Workshop* 17 (1984): 57-80; Mike Davis, "Why Is the U.S. Working Class Different," *New Left Review* 123 (1980): 5-44.

21. On Olmsted's paternalist credentials see Lewis Mumford, *The Brown Decades: A Study of the Arts in America, 1865-1895* (New York: Dover, 1955), 82-95; Julius Fabos, et al., *Frederick Law Olmsted Sr.: Founder of Landscape Architecture in America* (Amherst: University of Massachusetts Press, 1968).

22. Frederick Law Olmsted, *Creating Central Park, 1857-1861: The Papers of Frederick Law Olmsted*, vol. 3, ed. Charles Beveridge and David Schuyler (Baltimore: Johns Hopkins University Press, 1983). Hereafter all references to this six-volume collection will be cited by volume and page number in the text. Full information for each volume appears in the bibliography.

23. Philip S. Foner, *History of the Labor Movement in the United States*, vol. 1, *From Colonial Times to the Founding of the American Federation of Labor* (New York:

International, 1974), 147. Eric Hobsbawn describes a similar move a few years later by London capitalists who felt impending revolution and so precipitated a crisis in an effort to avoid one: "The very businessmen were desperate. It may in retrospect seem incomprehensible that businessmen . . . in the midst of their most dynamic period of expansion, should have been prepared to plunge their country into chaos, hunger and riot by a general political lock-out, merely in order to abolish tariffs. Yet in the terrible year 1841-42 it might well seem to the thoughtful capitalist that industry faced not merely inconvenience and loss, but general strangulation, unless the obstacles to further expansion were immediately removed" (*The Age of Revolution, 1789-1848* [New York: Weidenfield, 1962], 305). For more on Jackson and the Bank see George Rogers Taylor, *Jackson vs. Biddle: The Struggle over the Second Bank of the United States* (Boston: Heath, 1949). For more on labor organization during the Jacksonian era see Walter Hugins, *Jacksonian Democracy and the Working Class: A Study of the Workingman's Movement, 1829-1837* (Stanford: Stanford University Press, 1960).

24. See Hugins, *Jacksonian Democracy,* 63-68.

25. Quoted in P. Foner, *History of Labor,* 152.

26. See Hugins, *Jacksonian Democracy,* 51-80, 172-202.

27. Marvin E. Gettleman, *The Dorr Rebellion: A Study in American Radicalism, 1833-1849* (New York: Random House, 1973), xix.

28. George Templeton Strong, *The Diary of George Templeton Strong, Young Man in New York: 1835-1849,* edited by Allan Nevins and Milton Halsey Thomas (New York: Macmillan, 1952), 316; Anthony Gronowicz, *Race and Class Politics in New York City before the Civil War* (Boston: Northeastern University Press, 1998), 133.

29. Hobsbawm, *Revolution,* 305.

30. Sam Bass Warner, Jr. makes this point; see *The Urban Wilderness: A History of the American City* (New York: Harper and Row, 1972), 81.

31. Recently historians have pointed to the increase in grain on the world market after the Crimean War was settled and the fertile Hungarian plain began producing wheat as a global cause of the 1857 crisis. The global overproduction dramatically lowered the price of wheat in the United States and many farmers were unable to pay their debts. When depositors and foreign lenders came to the banks for money they found reserves utterly inadequate. See James Foreman-Peck, *A History of the World Economy: International Economic Relations since 1850* (Totowa, N.J.: Barnes and Noble Books, 1983), 84-85.

32. Quoted in Otto C. Lightner, *The History of Business Depressions: A Vivid Portrayal of Economic Adversity from the Beginning of Commerce to the Present* (New York: Burt Franklin, 1940), 142.

33. *History of Architecture and the Building Trades of Greater New York,* vol. 1 (New York: Union History Company, 1899), 153.

34. J. S. Gibbons, *The Banks of New York, Their Dealers, the Clearing House, and the Panic of 1857* (New York: Greenwood, 1968), 344.

35. *New York Times,* 8 October 1857.

36. Sacvan Bercovitch, *Office of the Scarlet Letter* Baltimore: Johns Hopkins University Press, 1991), xv. See also Larry J. Reynolds, *European Revolutions and the American Literary Renaissance* (New Haven: Yale University Press, 1988).

37. "The Rights of Labor," *Harper's Weekly* 1 (1857): 722.

38. For more on the "foreign" influence of labor and unemployed agitation during the Panic see, Franklin Folson, *Impatient Armies of the Poor: The Story of Collective Action of the Unemployed, 1808-1942* (Niwot, Colo.: University of Colorado Press, 1991), 85-86; P. Foner, *History of Labor*, 228-34. Folson also mentions municipal investment in Central Park as a means of diffusion (89). For more on the threatening and often violent action of workers and unemployed in 1857, see Folson, 83-107; *A Brief and Popular Account of the Panics and Revulsion in the U.S. from 1690-1857* (New York: Members of the New York Press, 1857); P. Foner, *History of Labor*, 219-48.

39. Harvey, *Urbanization*, 165.

40. While I will primarily be examining Frederick Law Olmsted and the details of the nineteenth-century park movement, I propose that my thesis has contemporary relevance. If pursuing such, one would want to examine the revival of interest in Olmsted's designs, including the establishment of his home as a national park in 1985.

41. See Roper, *FLO*, 127.

42. Michael A. Pagano and Ann O'M. Bowman, *Cityscapes and Capital: The Politics of Urban Development* (Baltimore: Johns Hopkins University Press, 1995), 71.

43. Quoted in P. Foner, *History of Labor*, 237.

44. *New York Times*, 3 November 1857.

45. Quoted in P. Foner, *History of Labor*, 239.

46. See Samuel Rezneck, *Business Depressions and Financial Panics: Essays in American Business and Economic History* (New York: Greenwood, 1985), 20.

47. *New York Herald*, 7 November 1857; quoted in Rozenzweig and Blackmar, *The Park*, 153.

48. David Schuyler, *The New Urban Landscape: The Redefinition of the City Form in Nineteenth-Century America* (Baltimore: Johns Hopkins University Press, 1986), 83.

49. Rozenzweig and Blackmar, *The Park*, 153.

50. Quoted in Rozenzweig and Blackmar, *The Park*, 174.

51. Rozenzweig and Blackmar, *The Park*, 150.

52. Rezneck, *Business Depressions*, 123-24.

53. Gronowicz, *Race and Class*, 94.

54. Charles Beveridge, *Frederick Law Olmsted: Designing the American Landscape* (New York: Rizzoli International, 1995), 136.

55. Frederick Law Olmsted, *The Papers of Frederick Law Olmsted*, Supplementary Series, vol. 1, *Writings on Public Parks, Parkways, and Park Systems*, ed. Charles Beveridge and Carolyn F. Hoffman (Baltimore: Johns Hopkins University Press, 1997), 483-84.

56. Henry Nash Smith's *Virgin Land: The American West as Symbol and Myth* (Cambridge, Mass.: Harvard University Press, 1950), remains the most useful description of the symbolic power of the Western landscape in the American imagination.

57. Friedrich Schiller, *On the Aesthetic Education of Man, In a Series of Letters*, trans. and ed. Elizabeth M. Wilkinson and L. A. Willoughby (Oxford: Clarendon Press, 1967), 25.

58. Schiller, *Aesthetic Education*, 17.

59. David Lloyd and Paul Thomas, *Culture and the State* (New York: Routledge, 1998), 47.

60. Raymond Williams, *Culture and Society: 1780-1950* (New York: Columbia University Press, 1958), 121.

61. Matthew Arnold, *Culture and Anarchy, with Friendship's Garland and Some Literary Essays*, ed. R. H. Super (Ann Arbor: University of Michigan Press, 1965), 135.

62. Lloyd and Thomas, *Culture*, 56.

63. Friedrich Schiller, "On the Stage as Moral Institution," in *Essays Aesthetical and Philosophical* (London: George Bell and Sons, 1879), quoted in Lloyd and Thomas, *Culture*, 56.

64. Lloyd and Thomas, *Culture*, 54-55.

65. Gina Crandell, *Nature Pictorialized: "The View" in Landscape History* (Baltimore: Johns Hopkins University Press, 1993), 5-6.

66. Quoted in Frederick Law Olmsted Jr., *Frederick Law Olmsted, Landscape Architect, 1822-1903* (New York: Blom, 1970), 263.

67. Stephen Crane, *Maggie: A Girl of the Streets* (New York: W.W. Norton, 1979), 10.

68. See Jeoffrey Blodgett, "Frederick Law Olmsted: Landscape Architecture as Conservative Reform," in *Art of the Olmsted Landscape*, ed. Bruce Kelly, et al. (New York: The Arts Publisher), 113.

69. Lee Hall, *Olmsted's America: An "Unpractical Man" and His Vision of Civilization* (Boston: Bullfinch, 1995), 48.

70. See Rozenzweig and Blackmar, *The Park*, 126-30.

71. It is unclear how Vaux and Olmsted became partners. They knew each other, but not closely. It seems likely that Vaux regarded Olmsted as well positioned to approve and contribute to the project. See Rozenzweig and Blackmar, *The Park*, 126-30.

72. On Vaux's abilities and on his relationship with Olmsted see Francis Kowsky, *Country, Park, and City: The Architecture and Life of Calvert Vaux* (New York: Oxford University Press, 1998).

73. Rozenzweig and Blackmar, *The Park*, 67.

74. David Sibley, *Geographies of Exclusion: Society and Difference in the West* (New York: Routledge, 1995), 32-48.

75. Frederick Law Olmsted to H. G. Stebbins, February 1872; quoted in Olmsted Jr., *Olmsted*, 263.

76. Olmsted to Henry G. Stebbins, 30 July 1873, Frederick Law Olmsted Papers, Manuscript Division, Library of Congress, Washington, D.C. (hereafter cited as FLOP).

77. Lloyd and Thomas, *Culture*, 125.

78. Roper, *FLO*, 130.

79. *New York Times*, 25 July 1856.

80. *New York Sun*, 5 October 1855.

81. Quoted in Rozenzweig and Blackmar, *The Park*, 64.

82. *New York Times*, 5 March 1856. Only about thirty percent of the inhabitants of Seneca Village were Irish—most were black (Rozenzweig and Blackmar, *The Park*, 66). Here, as in the previous long quote from the *Times*, the reporter reveals that race is primarily an effect of class. As Whitman suggested of his "sandy complexion'd" policeman, the Irish became the cops who criminalized the blacks, thereby helping to appropriate, in a negative manner, the privileges of whiteness for themselves. For more on the complex

manner by which the Irish appropriated whiteness, see Noel Ignatiev, *How the Irish Became White* (New York: Routledge, 1994).

83. Rozenzweig and Blackmar, *The Park,* 67.

84. Rozenzweig and Blackmar, *The Park,* 70.

85. Rozenzweig and Blackmar, *The Park,* 73.

86. Central Park was not a site of rioting until the Draft Riots of July 1863, when workers walked off the job to join an antidraft demonstration in the Park. See Rozenzweig and Blackmar, *The Park,* 195-96.

87. Rozenzweig and Blackmar, *The Park,* 91.

88. Frederick Law Olmsted to Rudolph Ulrich, 24 March 1892; quoted in Beveridge, *Designing,* 43.

89. Frederick Law Olmsted, *Justifying the Value of a Public Park,* 19; quoted in Beveridge, *Designing,* 50.

90. Frederick Law Olmsted, *Walks and Talks of an American Farmer* (New York: G. P. Putnam & Co., 1852), 64.

91. Olmsted, *Walks and Talks,* 64.

92. Frederick Law Olmsted, "Public Parks and the Enlargement of Towns," in *Civilizing American Cities: A Selection of Frederick Law Olmsted's Writings on City Landscapes* (Cambridge, Mass.: Harvard University Press, 1971), 96.

93. Horace Greeley, in *New York Tribune,* 30 January 1854.

94. Horace Greeley had a financial interest in the promotion of Nature and used his influential position to secure some profit from his investment. See the following chapter for a discussion of his relationship to Jay Cooke and Yellowstone National Park.

95. Quoted in Beveridge, *Designing,* 116.

96. Olmsted's most famous suburban project is Riverside, Illinois, designed in 1868. His success at defending elite space against "destructive" intrusions is revealed by Riverside's resistance to ghettoization.

97. Olmsted is obviously central to the history of the suburb in America. For more on his position in suburban history see John R. Stilgoe, *Borderland: Origins of the American Suburb, 1820-1939* (New Haven: Yale University Press, 1988), 223-71.

98. *New York Herald,* 5 May 1860.

99. See Rozenzweig and Blackmar, *The Park,* 212-25.

100. Rozenzweig and Blackmar, *The Park,* 215.

101. Edmund Leach, *Culture and Communication* (Cambridge: Cambridge University Press, 1976), 61.

102. Sibley, *Geographies,* 55.

103. See Elizabeth Blackmar, *Manhattan for Rent, 1758-1850* (Ithaca: Cornell University Press, 1989), 254-59.

104. Blackmar, *Manhattan,* 260.

105. Joel Schwartz, *The New York Approach: Robert Moses, Urban Liberals, and the Redevelopment of the Inner City* (Columbus: Ohio State University Press), 2.

106. Schwartz, *New York Approach,* 8.

107. Schwartz, *New York Approach,* 8-9.

108. Schwartz, *New York Approach,* 15.

Chapter Two: Olmsted's Failure

1. Intellectual and cultural historian Thomas Bender termed Olmsted and other republican reformers "the metropolitan gentry," men who used culture to gain status and leadership in a rapidly evolving social order. See Thomas Bender, *New York Intellects: A History of Intellectual Life in New York City, from 1750 to the Beginnings of Our Own Time* (Baltimore: Johns Hopkins University Press, 1987), 169-205.

2. Olmsted's departure from Central Park was facilitated by growing differences with the Park commission, especially member Andrew Haswell Green, who constantly badgered Olmsted about minor financial details. Olmsted, citing frustrations of authority and the prospect of a reduced role, offered his resignation from Park duties in January 1861.

3. Olmsted to Henry Bellows, 28 March 1861, FLOP.

4. *A Journey in the Seaboard Slave States, with Remarks on Their Economy* (New York: Dix, Edwards, 1856); *A Journey through Texas; or, a Saddle-Trip on the Southwestern Frontier: With a Statistical Appendix* (New York: Dix, Edwards, 1857); *A Journey in the Back Country* (New York: Mason Bros., 1860); *The Cotton Kingdom: A Traveller's Observations on Cotton and Slavery in the American Slave States* (New York: Mason Bros., 1861).

5. Arthur M. Schlesinger, "Editor's Introduction," xliii.

6. Olmsted to F. J. Kingsbury, June 1846. Schlesinger, xxxvii.

7. Olmsted, *Cotton*, 3.

8. Olmsted, *Cotton*, 4.

9. Frederick Law Olmsted, *New York Times,* 13 February 1854.

10. Frederick Law Olmsted, *New York Times,* 30 March 1853.

11. Olmsted, *Cotton*, 204.

12. Olmsted, *Cotton*, 160-61.

13. John Stuart Mill, *Considerations on Representative Government,* in *Essays on Politics and Society,* ed. John M. Robson; *Collected Works of John Stuart Mill,* vol. 19 (Toronto: University of Toronto Press, 1977), 394.

14. Mill, *Considerations*, 395.

15. Samuel Taylor Coleridge, *On the Constitution of the Church and State,* ed. John Colmer (Princeton: Princeton University Press, 1976), 67. On Mill's use of Coleridge see Raymond Williams, *Culture and Society: 1780-1950* (New York: Columbia University Press, 1958), 47-70.

16. Olmsted, *Cotton*, 513.

17. See *PFLO* I: 316-17.

18. *PFLO* I: 316-17.

19. Olmsted's propositions for the effective "cultivation" of freemen describe a militant education program. He suggests in *Cotton Kingdom* that slaves earn their freedom according to the Cuban model of emancipation, wherein slaves are free to purchase themselves at a regulated price. According to Olmsted, once free after such uncannily productive labor, the freemen would enter a system similar to that of the "reformatory punishment system, now in successful operation in some of the British penal colonies." The objective, Olmsted defers,

is simply to provide "the negroes an education in essential social morality, while they are drawing towards personal freedom" (*Cotton*, 199-200). Thus, even after purchasing freedom, the slave only "draws" towards it. Culture, for Olmsted, has a great deal of responsibility.

20. Henri Lefebvre, *The Production of Space* (Cambridge, Mass.: Blackwell, 1991), 280-81.

21. Alfred Runte, *Yosemite: The Embattled Wilderness* (Lincoln: University of Nebreaska Press, 1990), 15.

22. Runte, *Yosemite*, 13-27.

23. Mark Spence, "Dispossessing the Wilderness: Yosemite Indians and the National Park Ideal, 1864-1930," *Pacific Historical Review* (1996): 27-59.

24. Rebecca Solnit, *Savage Dreams: A Journey into the Hidden Wars of the American West* (San Francisco: Sierra Club Books, 1995).

25. Quoted in Solnit, *Savage Dreams*, 220.

26. Lafayette Bunnell, *Discovery of the Yosemite and the Indian War of 1851 Which Led to That Event* (Yosemite National Park: Yosemite Association, 1991), 213-14. While there are some footnote references by historians, Solnit's is the only critical engagement with Bunnell's text of which I am aware.

27. Solnit, *Savage Dreams*, 220.

28. As Mark Spence has noted, final Indian removal from Yosemite took place in the 1930s. The "Indian war of 1851," in which Bunnell participated, led to the relocation of Yosemite Indians to the San Joaquin Valley, but they immediately struggled to regain a place in the Yosemite Valley, with some success coming about two years after this original removal. See Mark Spence, "Dispossessing the Wilderness: Yosemite Indians and the National Park Ideal, 1864-1930," *Pacific Historical Review* (1996): 27-59; Runte, *Yosemite*, 10-12.

29. In 1990 the Yosemite Association reissued a very elegant edition of Bunnell's account, though they chose effectively to retitle it *Discovery of the Yosemite*, leaving off the rest of the original title (*and the Indian War of 1851 Which Led to That Event*) and persisting in the obfuscation of violence.

30. Olmsted's work with the Sanitary Commission remains the least considered aspect of his career, though it deserves a great deal of attention. I regret that this book, on the spatial, and "natural," deployments of culture does not offer the opportunity. For a review of Olmsted's work with the commission see Roper, *FLO*, 156-224.

31. Roper, *FLO*, 233.

32. Frederick Law Olmsted to John Olmsted, 20 August 1863, FLOP.

33. See Henry W. Bellows to Frederick Law Olmsted, 13 August 1863, FLOP.

34. Frederick Law Olmsted to Henry W. Bellows, 19 August 1863, FLOP.

35. Frederick Law Olmsted to Charles Loring Brace, 1 November 1884, FLOP.

36. Olmsted's labor "management" probably kept Mariposa viable longer than it otherwise would have been. The mines were simply at the wrong end of the lode and, combined with the estate's huge debt, could not be worked profitably enough to sustain the operation.

37. Horace Bushnell, "Barbarism the First Danger," in David L. Smith, ed., *Horace*

Bushnell: Selected Writings on Language, Religion, and American Culture (Chico, Calif.: Scholars Press, 1984), 155-158.

38. See Stephen Jay Gould, "The Politics of Evolution," *Psychohistory Review* 11 (1983): 15-35.

39. Olmsted to Hale, 21 October 1869; quoted in Robert Lewis, "Frontier and Civilization in the Thought of Frederick Law Olmsted," *American Quarterly* 29 (1977), 387:

40. Lewis, "Frontier," 385-403.

41. Henry Bellows, "Cities and Parks, with a Special Reference to the New York Central Park," *Atlantic Monthly* 7 (1861): 429. I have been fortunate to have at my easy disposal copies of such mainstream middle-brow journals as *Atlantic Monthly, Harper's Weekly,* and *Harper's Monthly* beginning with the very first issues. I was originally surprised by such extensive holdings at the relatively small and new university at which I did much of my research. I later noticed that the journals came from the libraries of the Calumet and Hecla Mining Company which operated in the area beginning in the mid-nineteenth century. A long and continuing history of labor disputes in the region suggests that the libraries were part of a socializing effort theorized, though probably not begun, by Olmsted. It bears mentioning the early issues are in very good, even mint, condition.

42. Peter Stallybrass and Allon White, *The Politics and Poetics of Transgression* (Ithaca: Cornell University Press, 1986), 97.

43. Here it is useful to point out a problem with one thinker who would appear useful in formulating a theory of public space, namely, Jurgen Habermas. What is most valuable in Habermas's thinking, according to my concerns about the repression of broad class identifications, is the attempt to figure how standards and values of justice might become universalized through a democratic process of unfettered communication. The principal problem confronting Habermas is precisely the spatial and temporal diversity of communities, or, ever proliferating localisms. The problem *with* Habermas, as P. Howell has suggested, is his "inability to think through the realities of differentiated political space." Harvey likewise comments, for "all his occasional references to material circumstances, [Habermas] treats the problem of communicative action as a linguistic discursive problem and consequently provides a very weak understanding of how the discursive 'moment' internalizes effects of power, material practices . . . and social relations." In short, according to my usage, Habermas lacks an adequate understanding of the ideological factors at work in constituted spaces. See P. Howell, "The Aspirations towards Universality in Political Theory and Political Geography," *Geoforum* 25 (1994): 423, 413-27; David Harvey, "From Space to Place and Back Again," in *Justice, Nature, and the Geography of Difference* (Cambridge, Mass.: Blackwell, 1996), 354, 334-65.

44. Alfred Runte, *National Parks: The American Experience* (Lincoln: University of Nebraska Press, 1987), 12.

45. I refer to the definition of hysteria developed in 1895 by Josef Breuer and Sigmund Freud, *Studies on Hysteria* (New York: Basic Books, 2000), see especially 85-6. The fullest discussion of Olmsted's emotional and somatic history appears in Melvin Kalfus, *Frederick Law Olmsted: The Passion of a Public Artist* (New York: New York University Press, 1990), 53-72.

46. See, for instance, Roger Starr, "The Motive behind Olmsted's Park," *The Public*

Interest 74 (1984): 66-76. Starr writes, a "chronicle of discontinuous careers, failures, or, at best, partial successes stands in sharp contrast to the achievements of Frederick Olmsted as the modern world perceives them" (68).

47. Stallybrass and White, *Politics*, 197.

48. J. H. Beadle, *The Undeveloped West* (Philadelphia: National Publishing, 1973), 381.

49. George Gwyther, M.D., "A Frontier Post and Country," *Overland Monthly and Out West Magazine* 5 (1870): 524.

50. Lawrence Barrett, "In the Track of a Great Race," *Overland Monthly and Out West Magazine* 3 (1869): 282.

51. Olmsted, *Texas*, 96.

52. Runte, *National Parks*, 12.

53. Quoted in Runte, *National Parks*, 19.

54. Runte, *National Parks*, 20.

Chapter Three: The (Over)Production of Place

1. Troy R. Johnson, *The Occupation of Alcatraz Island: Indian Self-Determination and the Rise of Native Activism* (Urbana: University of Illinois Press, 1996), 182.

2. Quoted in Johnson, *Alcatraz*, 192.

3. Johnson, *Alcatraz*, 201.

4. The period from the early 1870s to the mid-90s has been called the first "Great Depression"; see Eric Hobsbawm, *The Age of Extremes: A History of the World, 1914-1991* (New York: Pantheon Books, 1994), 87.

5. See Richard Slotkin, *Fatal Environment: The Myth of the Frontier in the Age of Industrialization, 1880-1890* (New York: Atheneum, 1985), 288; Walter T. K. Nugent, *Money and American Society, 1865-1880* (New York: Free Press, 1968), 177.

6. On the persistent preservationist view of Yellowstone see Alexander Wilson, *The Culture of Nature: North American Landscape from Disney to the Exxon Valdez* (Cambridge, Mass.: Blackwell Publishers, 1992), 224; Michael Bunce, *The Countryside Ideal: Anglo-American Images of Landscape* (New York: Routledge, 1994), 194.

7. See Patricia Nelson Limerick, "True West," *Yale Review* 75 (1986): 619-27; Sam B. Girgus, "Religious Freedom or Real Estate: The Problem of Ideology in Interdisciplinary Studies," *American Quarterly* 38 (1986): 299-304.

8. Henry Nash Smith, *Virgin Land: The American West as Symbol and Myth* (Cambridge, Mass.: Harvard University Press, 1950).

9. Lefebvre, *The Production of Space*, trans. Donald Nicholson-Smith (Cambridge, Mass.: Blackwell Publishers, 1991), 84.

10. The notion that the park functioned as an arena of and center for imperialist military activity is only now receiving attention; Mark David Spence has prepared a dissertation on native exclusion from the national parks which develops the history of military usage. See Mark David Spence, "Dispossessing the Wilderness: The Preservationist Ideal, Indian Removal, and National Parks" (Ph.D. diss., University of Southern California, 1996).

11. The interpretation of the Park as a reservation of "nature" is utterly common-place—I will be making reference to such views throughout the following. See especially Alfred Runte, *National Parks: The American Experience* (Lincoln: University of Nebraska Press, 1987); Aubrey L. Haines, *The Yellowstone Story: A History of Our First National Park*, vol. 1 (Niwot, Colo.: University of Colorado Press, 1996), 156-75.

12. Karl Marx, *Capital, Volume One* (New York: Penguin, 1990), 1059.

13. See William Cronon, *Changes in the Land: Indians, Colonists, and the Ecology of New England* (New York: Hill and Wang, 1983), 82-107.

14. As discussed in the previous chapters, this definition does not exhaust the complex meaning of the term "imperialism."

15. Marx, *Capital*, 304.

16. Lefebvre has been an important influence on David Harvey and other spatial theorists; in fact, it is precisely Lefebvre's notion of spatial production to which Harvey most is indebted. See Harvey *Justice*, 53, 241, 268, 272-74; Lefebvre, *Production* (Harvey, Afterword), 425-31. For comment on Harvey's use of Lefebvre see M. Gottdiener, *The Social Production of Urban Space* (Austin: University of Texas Press, 1985), xi-xiii; Michael Keith and Steve Pile, eds., *Place and the Politics of Identity* (New York: Routledge, 1993), 24-26.

17. Henri Lefebvre, "Space: Social Product and Use Value," in *Critical Sociology: European Perspectives*, ed. J. Freiberg (New York: Irvington Publishers, 1979), 288.

18. See Walter LaFeber, *The New Empire: An Interpretation of American Expansion, 1860-1898* (Ithaca: Cornell University Press, 1963), 8, 20, 230-40.

19. This is the principal thesis of LaFeber's influential study of U.S. imperialism in the nineteenth century (cited above). As discussed previously, it was also an idea entertained by both Hegel and Marx.

20. The term is Lauren Berlant's; I elaborate my use in the following. See Lauren Berlant, *The Anatomy of National Fantasy: Hawthorne, Utopia, and Everyday Life* (Chicago: University of Chicago Press, 1993), 20.

21. Patricia Hills, "Picturing Progress in the Era of Westward Expansion," in *The West as America: Reinterpreting Images of the Frontier, 1820-1920* (Washington, D.C.: Smithsonian Institution Press, 1991), 100.

22. I am finally less interested in landscape representations as cultural nationalism than as aspects of a complex and contradictory imperialism. Most discussions of the former tend to reify the works and ideas through a kind of self-referential contextualization rather than explicate through some description of social or economic function. This is especially true of Barbara Novak's highly regarded "contextualization" of nineteenth-century American landscape art, *Nature and Culture* (New York: Oxford University Press, 1980). Novak, like Hills, compares artists and their ideological representations to other cultural, which is to say equally ideological, figures.

23. Berlant, *Anatomy*, 20.

24. Jacques Lacan, *Ecrits: A Selection*, trans. Alan Sheridan (New York: W. W. Norton, 1977), 50.

25. Priscilla Wald, *Constituting Americans: Cultural Anxiety and Narrative Form* (Durham: Duke University Press, 1995), 299.

26. Wald, *Constituting Americans*, 2.

27. Homi Bhabha, "Of Mimicry and Man: The Ambivalence of Colonial Discourse," in *The Location of Culture* (New York: Routledge, 1994), 89.

28. Lefebvre, *Production*, 44.

29. Russell Means, *Where White Men Fear to Tread: The Autobiography of Russell Means* (New York: St. Martin's Press, 1995), 170.

30. Means, *Autobiography*, 168.

31. It is precisely the loss of this "indistinction" that so troubles many non-Indian Americans about gaming, and the attendant prosperity, on a few Indian reservations.

Chapter Four: The Nature of Violence

1. For a recent historical and rhetorical analysis of the ideal British countryside see Michael Bunce, *The Countryside Ideal: Anglo-American Images of the Landscape* (New York: Routledge, 1994), 5-76. See also Raymond Williams, *The Country and the City* (New York: Oxford University Press, 1973), especially, 1-8, 120-126.

2. Penn's is a figure properly contextualized in the "myth of the garden" skillfully elaborated—if not interrogated—by Henry Nash Smith and literally all others who focus on the landscape tradition in America. Rather than broadly examine the landscape tradition I will here consider particular people and representations tied to the Yellowstone region and the history of the national park idea. While I will refer to the symbology of the American landscape tradition my focus is not on landscape representation in general, but on the production of a particular nationalist place.

3. William Penn, "Some Account of the Province of Pennsylvania," in *William Penn and the Founding of Pennsylvania, 1680-1684: A Documentary History*, ed. Jean R. Soderlund (Philadelphia: University of Pennsylvania Press, 1983), 58.

4. Thomas Cole, *Thomas Cole's Poetry*, ed. Marshall B. Tymn (York, Penn.: Liberty Cap Books, 1972); quoted in Barbara Novak, *Nature and Culture: American Landscape Painting, 1825-1875* (New York: Oxford University Press, 1980), 157.

5. Angela Miller, *Empire of the Eye: Landscape Representation and American Cultural Politics, 1825-1875* (Ithaca: Cornell University Press, 1996), 44-49.

6. George Catlin, *Letters and Notes on the Manners, Customs, and Conditions of the North American Indians* (New York: Wiley and Putnam, 1842), 29.

7. Catlin, *Letters and Notes*, 29.

8. For his statement of mimetic transparency see, Catlin, *Notes*, 3. Catlin has been cited as a principal author of the dominant and romantic conceptualization of Plains Indians as "real Indians" though Jeffery Hanson notes that Catlin's "Choctaw Ball Game" shows the Choctaw living in tipis—a type of housing that would have been utterly impractical for Choctaw lifestyle (Jeffery Hanson, "Ethnicity and the Looking Glass: The Dialectics of National Indian Identity," *American Indian Quarterly* 21 [1997]: 199).

9. Indeed it glows still; despite exceeding brutality the "wild sons" have survived, persisting in their "sidelong looks." For a history of militant Native resurgence and repression since World War II see Russell Means, *Where White Men Fear to Tread: The*

Autobiography of Russell Means (New York: St. Martin's Press, 1995); Ward Churchill, *Agents of Repression: The F.B.I.'s Secret War Against the Black Panther Party and the American Indian Movement* (Boston: South End Press, 1986); Ward Churchill, *Struggle for the Land: A Land Rights Reader* (Monroe, Maine: Common Courage Press, 1993); M. Annette Jaimes, ed., *The State of Native America: Genocide, Colonization, and Resistance* (Boston: South End Press, 1992).

10. See Aubrey L. Haines, *The Yellowstone Story: A History of Our First National Park*, vol. 1 (Niwot, Colo.: University of Colorado Press, 1996), 8; Roderick Nash, *Wilderness and the American Mind* (New Haven: Yale University Press, 1967), 100.

11. Catlin, *Notes*, 294-295.

12. Gina Crandell, *Nature Pictorialized: "The View" in Landscape History* (Baltimore: Johns Hopkins University Press, 1993), 1.

13. William H. Goetzmann, *Army Exploration in the American West, 1803-1863* (Lincoln: University of Nebraska Press, 1979), 406.

14. Goetzmann, *Army Exploration*, 406.

15. William F. Raynolds, "Report of the Exploration of the Yellowstone and Missouri Rivers, in 1859-60," *S. Exec. Doc. 77*, 40th Congress, 1st session (1868); quoted in Kenneth H. Baldwin, ed., *Enchanted Enclosure: The Army Engineers and Yellowstone National Park, A Documentary History* (Washington, D.C.: U.S. Government Printing Office, 1976), 5.

16. Raynolds, "Report," 6.

17. *Helena Herald*, 29 July 1869; quoted in Haines, *Yellowstone Story*, 91.

18. Quoted in Haines, *Yellowstone Story*, 97.

19. Quoted in Haines, *Yellowstone Story*, 103. Whether Cook actually talked about a park or not is extremely questionable; whatever the case, he did not make a public case for it and was probably simply trying to gain credit well after the fact.

20. I am, of course, referring to Hawthorne's political dismissal from the Salem Custom House in 1848 that elicited in him such an antirevolutionary charge. The notion, developed by Sacvan Bercovitch and Larry Reynolds, that his most famous narrative (*The Scarlet Letter*), is indeed about containing a "red" scare, bears an important, though double, similarity to the spatial and narrative processes in which Langford was involved. See Sacvan Bercovitch, *The Office of the Scarlet Letter* (Baltimore: Johns Hopkins University Press, 1991); Larry Reynolds, *European Revolutions and the American Literary Renaissance* (New Haven: Yale University Press, 1988).

21. Haines, *Yellowstone Story*, 105.

22. Slason Thompson, *A Short History of American Railways, Covering Ten Decades* (New York: Appleton Press, 1925), 217.

23. Walter LaFeber, *The New Empire: An Interpretation of American Expansion, 1860-1898* (Ithaca: Cornell University Press, 1963), 31.

24. Thompson, *History*, 219.

25. Thompson, *History*, 217-18.

26. Thompson, *History*, 219.

27. Otto C. Lightner, *The History of Business Depressions: A Vivid Portrayal of Economic Adversity from the Beginnings of Commerce to the Present* (New York: Burt

Franklin, 1940), 160-61. Lightener goes on to point out that in the five years preceding the depression 2 billion dollars had been put into railroad expansion, an amount which "could not possibly bring an immediate return" and led directly to the Panic and depression (162-3).

28. Nathaniel P. Langford, *Diary of the Washburn Expedition to the Yellowstone and Firehole Rivers in the Year 1870* (St. Paul: F. J. Haynes, 1905), xiv.

29. Langford, *Diary*, xii.

30. Langford, *Diary*, xv.

31. Orrin H. and Lorraine Bonney, *Battle Drums and Geysers: The Life and Journals of Lt. Gustavus Cheyney Doane, Soldier and Explorer of the Yellowstone and Snake River Regions* (Chicago: Swallow Press, 1970), 23.

32. Quoted in Bonney, *Battle Drums,* 24.

33. The Marais River massacre remains one of the most unacknowledged episodes of gross violence in American history, though the Native American novelist James Welch gives an excellent imaginative rendering of the massacre and the events and lives surrounding it in his novel *Fools Crow* (New York: Viking, 1986), see especially 379-86.

34. Quoted in Bonney, *Battle Drums,* 22.

35. Recent studies of place in Heidegger have analyzed his complex relation and/or contribution to ecologism, see Anna Bramwell, *Blood and Soil: Walter Daare and Hitler's Green Party* (Buckinghamshire, England: Kensal Press, 1985); Ladelle McWhorter, ed., *Heidegger and the Earth: Essays in Environmental Philosophy* (Kirksville: Thomas Jefferson University Press, 1992), especially 1-33; Michael Zimmerman, "The Role of Spiritual Discipline in Learning to Dwell on Earth," in *Dwelling, Place, and Environment: Towards Phenomenology of Person and World,* ed. David Seamon and Robert Mugerauer (New York: Columbia University Press, 1989), 247-56.

36. Raymond Williams, *Resources of Hope: Culture, Democracy, Socialism* (New York: Verso, 1989), 321-22.

37. Williams, *Resources,* 29; I am indebted to David Harvey's discussion of Williams's complex notion of space in two essays reprinted in *Justice, Nature, and the Geography of Difference* (Cambridge, Mass.: Blackwell, 1996), "Militant Particularism and Global Ambition" (19-45), and "From Space to Place and Back Again" (291-328).

38. Williams's concept sounds suspiciously Heideggerian, yet there are important differences between the two thinkers' notions of place. For instance, Heidegger was terrified of the time-space compression he perceived in modern technological processes and sought quite consciously and deliberately to salvage and idealize the past in order formally, and, as we know, with rather authoritarian backing, to reinstitute "dwelling" in placeness. Williams shares neither Heidegger's attitude nor his relation to power. For more on place theory see David Harvey, "From Space to Place and Back Again," in *Justice,* 291-326; Y. Taun, *Space and Place: The Perspective of Experience* (Minneapolis: University of Minnesota Press, 1977).

39. As with many treaties, this one functioned without official ratification—the president never signed it. This relative commonality exclaims the "formality" of U.S./Native treaties. See U.S. Congress, Senate, Committee on Indian Affairs, *Crow Tribe of Indians of Montana,* S. Rpt. 463, 77th Congress, 1st session, 1942, 1.

40. Commissioner N. G. Taylor to Secretary of the Interior O. H. Browning, 18 April

1868, in *Annual Report of the Commissioner of Indian Affairs to the Secretary of Interior for the Year 1866* (Washington, D.C.: Government Printing Office, 1868), 196.

41. *Crow Tribe of Indians of Montana*, 3.

42. Louis Tuck Renz, *The History of the Northern Pacific Railroad* (Fairfield, Wash.: Galleon, 1980), 19.

43. Ellis Paxson Oberholtzer, *Jay Cooke: Financier of the Civil War*, vol. 2 (Philadelphia: G. W. Jacobs and Company, 1907), 169.

44. Oberholtzer, *Jay Cooke*, 170.

45. Jay Cooke to H. C. Fahnstock; quoted in Oberholtzer, *Cooke*, 226.

46. Raymond Williams, *Border Country* (London: Horizon, 1962), 291.

47. Langford, *Diary*, 6-7, 17, 92.

48. Nathaniel P. Langford, "The Wonders of Yellowstone," *Scribner's Monthly* 2, no. 1 (1871): 11.

49. He writes of Bozeman, a starting and supply point for Yellowstone expeditions, that it "is considered one of the most important prospective business locations in Montana. . . . Its inhabitants are patiently awaiting the time when the cars of the 'Northern Pacific' shall descend into their streets" (3).

50. Langford, "Wonders," 4, 7.

51. Langford, "Wonders," 6, 12.

52. Novak, *Nature and Culture*, 189.

53. Hiram M. Chittenden, *Yellowstone National Park, Historical and Descriptive*, revised ed. (Stanford: Stanford University Press, 1933), 6.

54. Chittenden, *Yellowstone*, 13.

55. Chittenden, *Yellowstone*, 12.

56. See Joyce E. Chaplin, "Natural Philosophy and an Early Racial Idiom in North America: Comparing English and Indian Bodies," *William and Mary Quarterly* 54 (1997): 33-43.

57. Quoted in Mark David Spence, "Dispossessing the Wilderness: The Preservationist Ideal, Indian Removal, and National Parks," Ph.D. diss., University of Southern California, 1996: epigraph.

58. Spence, "Preservationist Ideal," 118.

59. See Spence, "Preservationist Ideal," 212-45. For more on Indian use of the area see, Col. Wm. S. Brackett, "Indian Remains on the Upper Yellowstone," *Annual Report of the Board of Regents of the Smithsonian Institution* (Washington, D.C.: Smithsonian, 1892), 577-81; Haines, *Yellowstone Story*, 15-33; Joel C. Janetski, *Indians of Yellowstone Park* (Salt Lake City: University of Utah Press, 1987).

60. Spence, "Preservationist Ideal," 129.

61. Russell Osborne, *Journal of a Trapper; Or Nine Years Residence among the Rocky Mountains between the Years of 1834 and 1843*, ed. Aubrey L. Haines (Portland: Oregon Historical Society, 1955), 26-27.

62. See Spence, "Preservationist Ideal," 146; Haines, *Yellowstone Story*, 29.

63. Ken Burns and Stephen Ives, *The West*, distributed by Time-Life Video and Television, 1996. It is no small measure of Ken Burns's power that he has some of the past's most militant members of the Native sovereignty movement, like Russell Means and John

Trudell, working for him. Though I should also suggest that Russell Means's new employment is no great departure from his previous work for the Disney company in the animated film *Pocahontas*.

For some defeats other than that of Custer, see Dee Brown, *Fort Philip Kearny: An American Saga* (Lincoln: University of Nebraska Press, 1962), 184-90; Robert M. Utley, *Frontier Regulars: The United States Army and the Indian, 1866-1891* (Lincoln: University of Nebraska Press, 1973), 10-44, 93-110, 296-322.

64. These nations did not represent a unified force and fought each other as well as the U.S. military, and sometimes worked with the U.S. against traditional enemies. For instance, Crow scouts worked for Custer and Miles in their rather doomed campaigns against the Sioux and a loose affiliation of the remnants of other nations.

65. Edward P. Smith, *Report of the Commission to Negotiate with the Crow Tribe of Indians* (Washington, D.C.: Government Printing Office, 1873), 6.

66. William Ludlow, *Exploring Nature's Sanctuary: Captain William Ludlow's Report of Reconnaissance from Carroll, Montana Territory, on the Upper Missouri to the Yellowstone National Park, and Return Made in the Summer of 1875*, ed. Paul W. Taylor (Washington, D.C.: Government Printing Office, 1985), vi.

67. See Robert M. Utley, *Frontier Regulars: The United States Army and the Indian, 1866-1891* (Lincoln: University of Nebraska Press, 1973), 244.

68. Utley, *Frontier Regulars*, 242.

69. Charles P. Kindleberger, *Historical Economics: Art or Science?* (Berkeley: University of California Press, 1990); Walter T. K. Nugent, *Money and American Society, 1865-1880* (New York: Free Press, 1968), 264. I should note that though Jay Cooke's efforts did succeed in producing a park, the western rail expansion to the area was not completed until 1882, when the depression had somewhat abated.

70. Utley, *Frontier Regulars*, 247.

71. Richard Slotkin, *The Fatal Environment: The Myth of the Frontier in the Age of Industrialization, 1880-1890* (New York: Atheneum, 1985), 116.

72. For more on the "lukewarm" interest of the working class in western public lands see Helen S. Zahler, *Eastern Workingmen and National Land Policy, 1829-1862* (New York: Columbia University Press, 1944), 1-49.

73. *New York World*, 5 September 1875.

74. Slotkin, *Fatal Environment*, 6.

75. Slotkin, *Fatal Environment*, 286.

76. Slotkin, *Fatal Environment*, 286.

77. Slotkin, *Fatal Environment*, 286-87.

78. *The Northern Pacific Railroad; Its Route, Resources, Progress, and Business* (Philadelphia: Jay Cooke and Company, 1872), 4.

79. *Northern Pacific Railroad*, 4.

80. *Northern Pacific Railroad*, 7.

81. *Northern Pacific Railroad*, 9-10.

82. *Northern Pacific Railroad*, 20.

83. Matthew Josephson, *The Robber Barons: The Great American Capitalists, 1861-1901* (New York: Harcourt, Brace, 1934), 95. For Cooke and propaganda generally,

see Josephson, 93-99; M. Henrietta Larson, *Jay Cooke: Private Banker* (Cambridge, Mass.: Harvard University Press, 1936), 328-58.

84. Ludlow, *Nature's Sanctuary*, 19.

85. Raynolds, "Report," 6.

86. John W. Barlow, "Report of a Reconnaissance of the Basin of the Upper Yellowstone in 1871," in Baldwin, *Enchanted Enclosure*, 19.

87. For more on the first enterprises in the park see Richard A. Bartlett, *Yellowstone: A Wilderness Besieged* (Tucson: University of Arizona Press, 1985), especially 113-137.

88. See Gregory Evans Dowd, *A Spirited Resistance: The North American Indian Struggle for Unity, 1745-1815* (Baltimore: Johns Hopkins University Press, 1992).

89. Chittenden, *Yellowstone*, 98-99.

90. See Slotkin, *Fatal Environment*, 306-70 for more on the equation of Indians with urban workers.

91. U.S. Congress, *Yellowstone National Park Legislation*, S. 392, 42nd.

92. As the writing of one tourist demonstrates, the absence of a human past was essential to the experience of "discovery": "From [Yellowstone Lake's] unexplored inlets and coves the wild goose, duck, seagull, swan and pelican sail out their young broods, and moose, elk, bear and deer are permitted to live fearless lives and die natural deaths in regions yet untrodden by human feet" (Mary Bradshaw Richards, *A Trip to the Yellowstone, 1882* [Salt Lake City: University of Utah Press, 1994], 86).

93. Richards, *A Trip*, 20-21.

94. Richards, *A Trip*, 12.

95. Henri Lefebvre, *The Production of Space*, trans. Donald Nicholson-Smith (Cambridge, Mass.: Blackwell, 1991), 74.

96. Thomas Wentworth Higginson, ed., *Home Book of the Picturesque* (New York: G. P. Putnam, 1852), 1.

97. See Roper, *FLO*, 378-82.

98. On the 1857 suspension, see J. S. Gibbons, *The Banks of New York, Their Dealers, and the Clearing House, and the Panic of 1857* (New York: Greenwood, 1868), 343-99; Samuel Rezneck, *Business Depressions and Financial Panics: Essays in American Business and Economic History* (New York: Greenwood Press, 1985), 103-25. On the 1873 suspension, see Herman E. Kroos, ed., *Documentary History of Banking and Currency in the United States*, vol. 2 (New York: Chelsea House, 1969), 1601-1616.

Conclusion

1. Quoted in Roy Morris, Jr., *The Better Angel: Walt Whitman in the Civil War* (New York: Oxford University Press, 2000), 6.

2. *New York Times*, 5 January 1997.

3. *New York Times*, 5 January 1997.

4. Henri Lefebvre, *The Survival of Capitalism* (London: Allison and Busby, 1974), 21.

5. Neil Smith, "Antinomies of Space: Nature in Henri Lefebvre's *The Production of Space*," in *The Production of Public Space*, Andrew Light and Jonathan M. Smith, eds. (Lanham, Md.: Rowman & Littlefield, 1998).

6. Etienne Balibar, "'Rights of Man' and 'Rights of Citizen': The Modern Dialectic of Equality and Freedom," in *Masses, Classes, Ideas: Studies on Politics and Philosophy before and after Marx* (New York: Routledge, 1994), 41.

7. Balibar, "Rights," 41.

8. Balibar, "Rights," 43.

9. Balibar, "Rights," 44. Priscilla Wald has recently also used Balibar to attempt to explain how the paradoxical alliance of frequently "warring" factions has been formulated and preserved in the United States; see Wald, *Constituting*, 4-7.

10. Etienne Balibar, *The Philosophy of Marx*, trans. by Chris Turner (New York: Verso, 1995), 43. Here Balibar attempts to interrogate the Althusserian formulation of misrecognition by asking the difficult questions concerning derivation that Althusser left unresolved.

11. Balibar, *Marx*, 43.

12. Balibar, *Marx*, 51. In order to avoid confusion in what follows I should add here that the state, as I understand it, is not precisely synonymous with the nation. The former refers specifically to ruling interests, such that the state represents the collusion of political power and the dominant class. Nation refers to the invention of a "people" and is an ideological concept according to the definition I am formulating. The nation, to cite Balibar again, depends on the "projection of individual existence into the weft of a collective narrative, on the recognition of a common name and on traditions lived as the trace of an immemorial past (even when they have been fabricated and inculcated in the recent past)." Etienne Balibar, "The Nation Form: History and Ideology," in Balibar and Wallerstein, *Race, Nation, Class* (New York: Verso, 1991), 93.

Bibliography

Arnold, Matthew. *Culture and Anarchy.* Ann Arbor: University of Michigan Press, 1965.

Balibar, Etienne. "The Nation Form: History and Ideology." In *Race, Nation, Class: Ambiguous Identities,* by Immanuel Wallerstein and Etienne Balibar. New York: Verso, 1991.

———. *The Philosophy of Marx.* Translated by Chris Turner. New York: Verso, 1995.

———. "'Rights of Man' and 'Rights of Citizen': The Modern Dialectic of Equality and Freedom." In *Masses, Classes, Ideas: Studies on Politics and Philosophy before and after Marx.* New York: Routledge, 1994.

Baritz, Loren. "The Idea of the West." *American Historical Review* 46 (1961): 617-40.

Barlow, John W. "Report of a Reconnaissance of the Basin of the Upper Yellowstone in 1871." In *Enchanted Enclosure: The Army Engineers and Yellowstone National Park, A Documentary History.* Edited by Kenneth H. Baldwin. Washington, D.C.: U.S. Government Printing Office, 1976.

Barrett, Lawrence. "In the Track of a Great Race." *Overland Monthly and Out West Magazine* 3 (1869): 278-82.

Bartlett, Richard A. *Yellowstone: A Wilderness Besieged.* Tucson: University of Arizona Press, 1985.

Bataille, Georges. *The Accursed Share: An Essay in General Economy.* Translated by Robert Hurley. New York: Zone Books, 1988.

Baudet, Henri. *Paradise on Earth: Some Thoughts on European Images of Non-European Man.* New Haven: Yale University Press, 1965.

Beadle, J. H. *The Undeveloped West.* Philadelphia: National, 1873.

Bellows, Henry. "Cities and Parks, with a Special Reference to the New York Central Park." *Atlantic Monthly* 7 (1861): 416-29.

Bender, Thomas. *New York Intellects: A History of Intellectual Life in New York City, from 1750 to the Beginnings of Our Own Time.* Baltimore: Johns Hopkins University Press, 1997.

———. *Toward an Urban Vision: Ideas and Institutions in Nineteenth-Century America.* Lexington: University Press of Kentucky, 1975.

Bercovitch, Sacvan. *The Office of the Scarlet Letter*. Baltimore: Johns Hopkins University Press, 1991.

Berlant, Lauren. *The Anatomy of National Fantasy: Hawthorne, Utopia, and Everyday Life*. Chicago: University of Chicago Press, 1993.

Beveridge, Charles E. *Frederick Law Olmsted: Designing the American Landscape*. New York: Rizzoli International, 1995.

———. "Frederick Law Olmsted's Theory of Landscape Design." *Nineteenth Century* 3 (1977): 38-43.

Bhabha, Homi. *The Location of Culture*. New York: Routledge, 1994.

Blackmar, Elizabeth. *Manhattan for Rent, 1758-1850*. Ithaca: Cornell University Press, 1989.

Blodgett, Jeoffrey. "Frederick Law Olmsted: Landscape Architecture as Conservative Reform." *Journal of American History* 62 (1976): 869-89.

Blumin, Stuart. *The Emergence of the Middle Class: Social Experience in the American City, 1760-1900*. Cambridge, Mass.: Harvard University Press, 1989.

Bonney, Orrin H., and Lorraine Bonney. *Battle Drums and Geysers: The Life and Journals of Lt. Gustavus Cheyney Doane, Soldier and Explorer of the Yellowstone and Snake River Regions*. Chicago: Swallow Press, 1970.

Brackett, Col. Wm. S. "Indian Remains on the Upper Yellowstone." In *Annual Report of the Board of Regents of the Smithsonian Institution*. Washington, D.C.: Smithsonian Institution Press, 1982.

Bramwell, Anna. *Blood and Soil: Walter Daare and Hitler's Green Party*. Buckinghamshire, England: Kensal Press, 1985.

Breuer, Josef, and Sigmund Freud. *Studies on Hysteria*. New York: Basic Books, 2000.

A Brief and Popular Account of the Panics and Revulsion in the U.S. from 1690-1857. New York: Members of the New York Press, 1857.

Brown, Dee. *Fort Philip Kearny: An American Saga*. Lincoln: University of Nebraska Press, 1962.

Bunce, Michael. *The Countryside Ideal: Anglo-American Images of Landscape*. New York: Routledge, 1994.

Bunnell, Lafayette. *Discovery of the Yosemite and the Indian War of 1851 Which Led to That Event*. Los Angeles: G.W. Gerlicher, 1880. Reprint, Yosemite National Park, Calif.: Yosemite Association, 1991.

Burke, Edmund. *A Philosophical Inquiry into the Origin of Our Ideas of the Sublime and the Beautiful*. New York: Oxford University Press, 1990.

Burns, Ken. *The West*. Time-Life Video and Television, 1996.

Bushnell, Horace. "Barbarism the First Danger." In *Horace Bushnell: Selected Writings on Language, Religion, and American Culture*. Edited by David L. Smith. Chico, Calif.: Scholars Press, 1984.

Capie, Forrest, and Geoffrey E. Wood, eds. *Financial Crisis and the World Banking System*. New York: St. Martin's Press, 1986.

Catlin, George. *Letters and Notes on the Manners, Customs, and Conditions of the North American Indians*, 2nd ed. New York: Wiley and Putnam, 1842.

Chaplin, Joyce E. "Natural Philosophy and Early Racial Idiom in North America: Comparing English and Indian Bodies." *William and Mary Quarterly* 54 (1997): 33-43.

Chittenden, Hiram M. *Yellowstone National Park, Historical and Descriptive*. Revised ed. Stanford: Stanford University Press, 1933.

Churchill, Ward. *Agents of Repression: The F.B.I.'s Secret War against the Black Panther Party and the American Indian Movement*. Boston: South End Press, 1992.

———. *Struggle for the Land: A Land Rights Reader*. Monroe, Maine: Common Courage Press, 1993.

Churchill, Ward, and Winona LaDuke. "Native North America: The Political Economy of Radioactive Colonialism." In *The State of Native America: Genocide, Colonization, and Resistance*. Edited by Annette Jaimes. Boston: South End Press, 1992.

Cole, Thomas. *Thomas Cole's Poetry*. Edited by Marshall B. Tymn. York, Penn.: Liberty Cap Books, 1972.

Coleridge, Samuel Taylor. *On the Constitution of the Church and State*. Edited by John Colmer. Princeton: Princeton University Press, 1976.

Crandell, Gina. *Nature Pictorialized: "The View" in Landscape History*. Baltimore: Johns Hopkins University Press, 1993.

Crane, Stephen. *Maggie: A Girl of the Streets*. New York: W.W. Norton , 1979.

Cronon, William. *Changes in the Land: Indians, Colonists, and the Ecology of New England*. New York: Hill and Wang, 1983.

Davis, Mike. "Why Is the U.S. Working Class Different?" *New Left Review* 123 (1980): 5-44.

Donaldson, Elizabeth J. "Picturesque Scenes, Sentimental Creatures: The Rhetoric and Politics of American Nature Writing, 1890-1920." Ph.D. diss., The State University of New York at Stony Brook, 1997.

Dowd, Gregory Evans. *A Spirited Resistance: The North American Indian Struggle for Unity, 1745-1815*. Baltimore: Johns Hopkins University Press, 1992.

Dunn, Richard S., and Mary Maples, ed. *The World of William Penn*. Philadelphia: University of Pennsylvania Press, 1986.

Echeverria, Durand. *Mirage in the West: A History of the French Image of American Society to 1815*. Princeton: Princeton University Press, 1957.

Emmons, David E. *The Butte Irish: Class and Ethnicity in an American Mining Town*. Urbana: University of Illinois Press, 1990.

Evernden, Neil. *The Social Creation of Nature*. Baltimore: Johns Hopkins University Press, 1992.

Fabos, Julius, et al. *Frederick Law Olmsted Sr.: Founder of Landscape Architecture in America*. Amherst: University of Massachusetts Press, 1968.

Fein, Albert, ed. *Landscape into Cityscape: Frederick Law Olmsted's Plan for a Greater New York City*. Ithaca: Cornell University Press, 1968.

Fiedler, Leslie. *Love and Death in the American Novel*. New York: Stein and Day, 1960.

Folson, Franklin. *Impatient Armies of the Poor: The Story of Collective Action of the Unemployed, 1808-1942*. Niwot, Colo.: University of Colorado Press, 1991.

Foner, Eric. "Why Is There No Socialism in America?" *History Workshop* 17 (1984): 57-80.

Foner, Philip S. *History of the Labor Movement in the United States*. Vol. 1, *From Colonial Times to the Founding of the American Federation of Labor*. New York: International, 1974.

Foreman-Peck, James. *A History of the World Economy: International Economic Relations*

Since 1850. Totowa, N.J.: Barnes and Noble, 1983.

Foucault, Michel. "Of Other Spaces." *Diacritics* 16:1 (1986): 22-27.

Gettleman, Marvin E. *The Dorr Rebellion: A Study in American Radicalism, 1833-1849*. New York: Random House, 1973.

Gibbons, J. S. *The Banks of New York, Their Dealers, and the Clearing House, and the Panic of 1857*. New York: Greenwood, 1968.

Giddens, Anthony. *The Constitution of Society*. Cambridge, Mass.: Polity, 1984.

Girgus, Sam B. "Religious Freedom or Real Estate: The Problem of Ideology in Interdisciplinary Studies." *American Quarterly* 38 (1986): 299-304.

Goetzmann, William H. *Army Exploration in the American West, 1803-1863*. Lincoln: University of Nebraska Press, 1979.

Gottdiener, M. *The Social Production of Urban Space*. 2nd ed. Austin: University of Texas Press, 1985.

Gould, Stephen Jay. "The Politics of Evolution." *Psychohistory Review* 11 (1983): 15-35.

Greeley, Horace. *New York Times*. 30 January 1854.

Greene, Jack P. *The Intellectual Construction of America: Exceptionalism and Identity from 1492 to 1800*. Chapel Hill: University of North Carolina Press, 1993.

Gregory, Derek. *Geographical Imaginations*. New York: Blackwell, 1994.

Gronowicz, Anthony. *Race and Class Politics in New York City before the Civil War*. Boston: Northeastern University Press, 1998.

Gwyther, George. "A Frontier Post and Country." *Overland Monthly and Out West Magazine* 5 (1870): 520-26.

Haines, Aubrey L. *The Yellowstone Story: A History of Our First National Park*. Vol. 1. Niwot, Colo.: University Press of Colorado, 1996.

Hall, Lee. *Olmsted's America: An "Unpractical Man" and His Vision of Civilization*. Boston: Bullfinch, 1995.

Hanson, Jeffery. "Ethnicity and the Looking Glass: The Dialectics of National Indian Identity." *American Indian Quarterly* 21 (1997): 195-208.

Harvey, David. "Class Relations, Social Justice, and the Political Geography of Difference." In *Place and the Politics of Identity*. Edited by Michael Keith and Steve Pile, 41-66. New York: Routledge, 1993.

———. "Dialectics." In *Justice, Nature, and the Geography of Difference*. Cambridge, Mass.: Blackwell, 1996.

———. "From Space to Place and Back Again." In *Justice, Nature, and the Geography of Difference*. Cambridge, Mass.: Blackwell, 1996.

———. *Justice, Nature, and the Geography of Difference*. Cambridge, Mass.: Blackwell, 1996.

———. "Militant Particularism and Global Ambition." In *Justice, Nature, and the Geography of Difference*. Cambridge, Mass.: Blackwell, 1996.

———. *The Urbanization of Capital*. Baltimore: Johns Hopkins University Press, 1985.

Hawkins, Kenneth Blair. "The Therapeutic Landscape: Nature, Architecture, and Mind in Nineteenth-Century America." Ph.D. diss., University of Rochester, 1991.

Hegel, Georg Wilhelm Friedrich. *The Philosophy of History*. Translated by J. Sibree. New York: Dover, 1956.

———. *The Philosophy of Right.* Translated by T. M. Knox. New York: Dover, 1956.

Higginson, Thomas Wentworth, ed. *Home Book of the Picturesque.* New York: G. P. Putnam, 1852.

Hills, Patricia. "Picturing Progress in the Era of Westward Expansion." In *The West as America: Reinterpreting Images of the Frontier, 1820-1920.* Edited by William H. Truettner. Washington, D.C.: Smithsonian Institution Press, 1991.

History of Architecture and the Building Trades of Greater New York. Vol 1. New York: Union History Company: 1899.

Hobsbawm, Eric. *The Age of Extremes: A History of the World, 1914-1991.* New York: Pantheon, 1994.

———. *The Age of Revolution, 1789-1848.* New York: Weidenfield, 1962.

Howell, P. "The Aspirations toward Universality in Political Theory and Political Geography." *Geoforum* 24 (1994): 413-27.

Hugins, Walter. *Jacksonian Democracy and the Working Class: A Study of the Workingman's Movement, 1829-1837.* Stanford: Stanford University Press, 1960.

Ignatiev, Noel. *How the Irish Became White.* New York: Routledge, 1994.

Jaimes, Annette, ed. *The State of Native America: Genocide, Colonization, and Resistance.* Boston: South End Press, 1992.

Janetski, Joel C. *Indians of Yellowstone Park.* Salt Lake City: University of Utah Press, 1987.

Jefferson, Thomas. *Notes on the State of Virginia.* New York: Torchbooks, 1964.

Johnson, Troy R. *The Occupation of Alcatraz Island: Indian Self-Determination and the Rise of Native Activism.* Urbana: University of Illinois Press, 1996.

Josephson, Matthew. *The Robber Barons: The Great American Capitalists, 1861-1901.* New York: Harcourt, Brace, 1934.

Kalfus, Melvin. *Frederick Law Olmsted: The Passion of a Public Artist.* New York: New York University Press, 1990.

Katzneson, Ira, and Aristide R. Zolberg. *Working-Class Formation.* Princeton: Princeton University Press, 1986.

Keith, Michael, and Steve Pile, eds. *Place and the Politics of Identity.* New York: Routledge, 1993.

Kindleberger, Charles P. *Historical Economics: Art or Science?* Berkeley: University of California Press, 1990.

———. *Manias, Panics, and Crashes: A History of Financial Crises.* New York: Basic Books, 1978.

Kowsky, Francis. *Country, Park, and City: The Architecture and Life of Calvert Vaux.* New York: Oxford University Press, 1998.

Kroos, Herman E., ed. *Documentary History of Banking and Currency in the United States.* Vol. 2. New York: Chelsea House, 1969.

Lacan, Jacques. *Ecrits: A Selection.* Translated by Alan Sheridan. New York: W. W. Norton, 1977.

LaFeber, Walter. *The New Empire: An Interpretation of American Expansion, 1860-1898.* Ithaca: Cornell University Press, 1963.

Langford, Nathaniel P. *Diary of the Washburn Expedition to the Yellowstone and Firehole Rivers in the Year 1870.* St. Paul: F. J. Haynes, 1905.

———. "The Wonders of Yellowstone." *Scribner's Monthly* 2, no. 1 (1871): 1-20.

Larson, Henrietta. *Jay Cooke: Private Banker.* Cambridge, Mass.: Harvard University Press, 1936.

Leach, Edmund. *Culture and Communication.* Cambridge: Cambridge University Press, 1976.

Lefebvre, Henri. *The Production of Space.* Translated by Donald Nicholson-Smith. Cambridge, Mass.: Blackwell, 1991.

———. "Space: Social Product and Use Value." In *Critical Sociology: European Perspectives.* Edited by J. Freiberg. New York: Irvington, 1979.

———. *The Survival of Capitalism.* London: Allison and Busby, 1974.

Lewis, Robert. "Frontier and Civilization in the Thought of Frederick Law Olmsted." *American Quarterly* 29 (1977): 385-403.

Lightner, Otto C. *The History of Business Depressions: A Vivid Portrayal of Economic Adversity from the Beginnings of Commerce to the Present.* New York: Burt Franklin, 1940.

Limerick, Patricia Nelson. "True West." *Yale Review* 75 (1986): 619-27.

Lloyd, David, and Paul Thomas. *Culture and the State.* New York: Routledge, 1998.

Ludlow, William. *Exploring Nature's Sanctuary: Captain William Ludlow's Report of Reconnaissance from Carroll, Montana Territory, on the Upper Missouri to the Yellowstone National Park, and Return Made in the Summer of 1875.* Edited by Paul W. Taylor. Washington, D.C.: U.S. Government Printing Office, 1985.

Marx, Karl. *Capital: Volume One.* New York: Penguin, 1990.

McKinsey, Elizabeth. *Niagra Falls: Icon of the American Sublime.* Cambridge: Cambridge University Press, 1985.

McWhorter, Ladelle, ed. *Heidegger and the Earth: Essays in Environmental Philosophy.* Kirksville: Thomas Jefferson University Press, 1992.

Means, Russell. *Where White Men Fear to Tread: The Autobiography of Russell Means.* New York: St. Martin's Press, 1995.

Mill, John Stuart. *Collected Works of John Stuart Mill.* Edited by John M. Robson. Vol. 19, *Considerations on Representative Government.* Toronto: University of Toronto Press, 1977.

Miller, Angela. *Empire of the Eye: Landscape Representation and American Cultural Politics, 1825-1875.* Ithaca: Cornell University Press, 1996.

Mitchell, Brian C. *The Paddy Camps: The Irish of Lowell, 1821-61.* Urbana: University of Illinois Press, 1988.

Minsky, Hyman P. "Financial Stability Revisited: The Economics of Disaster." In *Reappraisal of the Federal Reserve Discount Mechanism.* Washington D.C.: U.S. Government Printing Office, 1972.

More, Sir Thomas. *Utopia.* In *The Complete Works of Sir Thomas More.* Edited by Edward Surtz and J. H. Hexter, 4 vols. New Haven: Yale University Press, 1965.

Morris, Roy, Jr. *The Better Angel: Walt Whitman in the Civil War.* New York: Oxford University Press, 2000.

Mosher, Anne E. "Capital Transformation and the Restructuring of Place: The Creation of a Model Industrial Town." Ph.D. diss., Pennsylvania State University, 1989.

Mumford, Lewis. *The Brown Decades: A Study of the Arts in America, 1865-1895.* New York: Dover, 1955.

Nash, Roderick. *Wilderness and the American Mind*. New Haven: Yale University Press, 1967.

Newton, Norman T. *Design on the Land: The Development of Landscape Architecture*. Cambridge, Mass.: Harvard University Press, 1971.

Northern Pacific Railroad: Its Route, Resources, Progress, and Business. Philadelphia: Jay Cooke, 1872.

Novak, Barbara. *Nature and Culture: American Landscape Painting, 1825-1875*. New York: Oxford University Press, 1980.

Nugent, Walter T. K. *Money and American Society, 1865-1880*. New York: Free Press, 1968.

Oberholtzer, Ellis Paxson. *Jay Cooke: Financier of the Civil War*. Vol. 2. Philadelphia: G. W. Jacobs, 1907.

Olmsted, Frederick Law. *Civilizing American Cities: A Selection of Frederick Law Olmsted's Writings on City Landscapes*. Cambridge, Mass.: Harvard University Press, 1971.

———. *The Cotton Kingdom: A Traveller's Observations on Cotton and Slavery in the American Slave States*. Edited by Arthur M. Schlesinger. New York: Mason Brothers, 1861.

———. *A Journey in the Back Country*. New York: Mason Brothers, 1860.

———. *A Journey in the Seaboard Slave States, with Remarks on Their Economy*. New York: Dix, Edwards, 1857.

———. *A Journey through Texas; or, a Saddle-Trip on the Southwestern Frontier; with a Statistical Appendix*. New York: Dix, Edwards, 1857.

———. *The Papers of Frederick Law Olmsted*. Edited by Charles E. Beveridge and Davis Schuyler. Vol. 3, *Creating Central Park, 1857-1861*. Baltimore: Johns Hopkins University Press, 1983.

———. *The Papers of Frederick Law Olmsted*. Edited by Victoria Post Ranney. Vol. 5, *The California Frontier, 1863-1865*. Baltimore: Johns Hopkins University Press, 1990.

———. *The Papers of Frederick Law Olmsted*. Edited by David Schuyler and Jane Turner Censer. Vol. 6, *The Years of Olmsted, Vaux, and Company, 1865-1874*. Baltimore: Johns Hopkins University Press, 1992.

———. *The Papers of Frederick Law Olmsted, Supplementary Series*. Edited by Charles Beveridge and Carolyn F. Hoffman. Vol. 1, *Writings on Public Parks, Parkways, and Park Systems*. Baltimore: Johns Hopkins University Press, 1997.

———. *Walks and Talks of an American Farmer*. New York: Putnam, 1852.

Olmsted, Frederick Law, Jr. *Frederick Law Olmsted: Landscape Architect, 1822-1903*. New York: Blom, 1970.

Olwig, Kenneth R. "Reinventing Common Nature: Yosemite and Mt. Rushmore—A Meandering Tale of Double Nature." In *Uncommon Ground: Rethinking the Human Place in Nature*. Edited by William Cronon. New York: W. W. Norton, 1996.

Osborne, Russell. *Journal of a Trapper; Or Nine Years Residence among the Rocky Mountains between the Years 1834 and 1843*. Edited by Aubrey L. Haines. Portland: Oregon Historical Society, 1955.

Pagano, Michael, and Ann O'M. Bowman. *Cityscapes and Capital: The Politics of Urban Development*. Baltimore: Johns Hopkins University Press, 1995.

Penn, William. "Some Account of the Province of Pennsylvania." In *William Penn and the Founding of Pennsylvania, 1680-1684: A Documentary History*. Edited by Jean R. Soderlund. Philadelphia: University of Pennsylvania Press, 1983.

Raynolds, William F. "Report of the Exploration of the Yellowstone and Missouri Rivers." In *Enchanted Enclosure: The Army Engineers and Yellowstone National Park, a Documentary History*. Edited by Kenneth H. Baldwin. Washington, D.C.: U.S. Government Printing Office, 1976.

Renz, Louis Tuck. *The History of the Northern Pacific Railroad*. Fairfield, Wash.: Galleon, 1980.

Reynolds, Larry J. *European Revolutions and the American Literary Renaissance*. New Haven: Yale University Press, 1988.

Rezneck, Samuel. *Business Depressions and Financial Panics: Essays in American Business and Economic History*. New York: Greenwood, 1985.

Richards, Mary Bradshaw. *A Trip to the Yellowstone, 1882*. Salt Lake City: University of Utah Press, 1994.

Ridge, Martin. "Ray Allen Billington, Western History, and American Exceptionalism." *Pacific Historical Review* 56 (1987): 495-511.

"The Rights of Labor." *Harper's Weekly* 1 (1857): 722.

Roediger, David R. *The Wages of Whiteness: Race and the Making of the American Working Class*. New York: Verso, 1991.

Roper, Laura Wood. *FLO: A Biography of Frederick Law Olmsted*. Baltimore: Johns Hopkins University Press, 1973.

Rozenzweig, Roy, and Elizabeth Blackmar. *The Park and the People: A History of Central Park*. Ithaca: Cornell University Press, 1992.

Runte, Alfred. *National Parks: The American Experience*. Lincoln: University of Nebraska Press, 1987.

———. *Yosemite: The Embattled Wilderness*. Lincoln: University of Nebraska Press, 1990.

Schiller, Friedrich. *On the Aesthetic Education of Man, in a Series of Letters*. Translated and edited by Elizabeth M. Wilkinson and L. A. Willoughby. Oxford: Clarendon Press, 1967.

———. "On the Stage as Moral Institution." In *Essays Aesthetical and Philosophical*. London: George Bell and Sons, 1879.

Schuyler, David. *The New Urban Landscape: The Redefinition of the City Form in Nineteenth-Century America*. Baltimore: Johns Hopkins University Press, 1986.

Schwartz, Joel. *The New York Approach: Robert Moses, Urban Liberals, and the Redevelopment of the Inner City*. Columbus: Ohio State University Press, 1992.

Shafer, Byron E., ed. *Is America Different? A New Look at American Exceptionalism*. Oxford: Clarendon, 1991.

Shalev, Michael, and Walter Korpi. "Working-Class Mobilization and American Exceptionalism." *Economic and Industrial Democracy* 1 (1980): 31-61.

Sibley, David. *Geographies of Exclusion: Society and Difference in the West*. New York: Routledge, 1995.

Slotkin, Richard. *Fatal Environment: The Myth of the Frontier in the Age of Industrialization, 1880-1890*. New York: Atheneum, 1985.

———. *Regeneration through Violence: The Mythology of the American Frontier*. Middletown: Wesleyan University Press, 1973.

Smith, Edward P. *Report of the Commission to Negotiate with the Crow Tribe of Indians*. Washington, D.C.: U.S. Government Printing Office, 1873.

Smith, Henry Nash. *Virgin Land: The American West as Symbol and Myth*. Cambridge, Mass.: Harvard University Press, 1950.

Smith, Neil. "Antinomies of Space: Nature in Henri Lefebvre's *The Production of Space*." In *The Production of Public Space*. Edited by Andrew Light and Jonathan M. Smith. Lanham, Md.: Rowman and Littlefield, 1998.

Soja, Edward. *Postmodern Geographies: The Reassertion of Space in Critical Theory*. London: Verso, 1989.

Solnit, Rebecca. *Savage Dreams: A Journey into the Hidden Wars of the American West*. San Francisco: Sierra Club Books, 1994.

Sombart, Werner. *Why Is there No Socialism in the United States?* Translated by Patricia M. Hocking and C. T. Husbands. New York: M. E. Sharpe, 1906.

Spence, Mark David. "Crown of the Continent, Backbone of the World: The American Wilderness Ideal and Blackfeet Exclusion from Glacier National Park." *Environmental History* 1 (1996): 29-49.

———. *Dispossessing the Wilderness: Indian Removal and the Making of the National Parks*. New York: Oxford University Press, 1999.

———. "Dispossessing the Wilderness: The Preservationist Ideal, Indian Removal, and National Parks." Ph.D. diss., University of Southern California, 1996.

———. "Dispossessing the Wilderness: Yosemite Indians and the National Park Ideal, 1864-1930." *Pacific Historical Review* 64 (1996): 27-59.

Stallybrass, Peter, and Allon White. *The Politics and Poetics of Transgression*. Ithaca: Cornell University Press, 1986.

Starr, Roger. "The Motive behind Olmsted's Park." *Public Interest* 74 (1984): 66-76.

Stilgoe, John R. *Borderland: Origins of the American Suburb, 1820-1939*. New Haven: Yale University Press, 1988.

Strong, George Templeton. *The Diary of George Templeton Strong, Young Man in New York: 1835-1849*. Edited by Allan Nevins and Milton Halsey Thomas. New York: Macmillan, 1952.

Taun, Y. *Space and Place: The Perspective of Experience*. Minneapolis: University of Minnesota Press, 1977.

Taylor, George Rogers. *Jackson vs. Biddle: The Struggle over the Second Bank of the United States*. Boston: Heath, 1949.

Taylor, N. G. *Annual Report of the Commissioner of Indian Affairs to the Secretary of the Interior for the Year 1866*. Washington, D.C.: U.S. Government Printing Office, 1868.

Thompson, Slason. *A Short History of American Railways, Covering Ten Decades*. New York: Appleton Press, 1925.

Tocqueville, Alexis de. *Democracy in America*. New York: Vintage, 1990.

Union History Company. *History of Architecture and the Building Trades of Greater New York*. Vol. 1. New York: Union History Company, 1899.

U.S. Congress. Senate. Committee on Indian Affairs. *Crow Tribe of Indians of Montana*. 77th Cong., 1st sess., 1942, Senate Report 463.

———. *Yellowstone National Park Legislation*. 42nd Cong., 2nd sess., 1872, Senate Report 392.

Utley, Robert M. *Frontier Regulars: The United States Army and the Indian, 1866-1891*.

Lincoln: University of Nebraska Press, 1973.

Wald, Priscilla. *Constituting Americans: Cultural Anxiety and Narrative Form*. Durham: Duke University Press, 1995.

Warner, Sam Bass, Jr. *The Urban Wilderness: A History of the American City*. New York: Harper and Row, 1972.

Welch, James. *Fools Crow*. New York: Viking, 1986.

White, Eugene N., ed. *Crashes and Panics: The Lessons from History*. Homewood, Ill.: Dow Jones, 1990.

Whitman, Walt. "Specimen Days." In *Complete Prose Works*. Philadelphia: David McKay, 1897.

Wilentz, Sean. *Chants Democratic: New York City and the Rise of the Working Class, 1788-1850*. New York: Oxford University Press, 1984.

Williams, Raymond. *Border Country*. London: Horizon Press, 1962.

————. *The Country and the City*. New York: Oxford University Press, 1973.

————. *Culture and Society: 1780-1950*. New York: Columbia University Press, 1958.

————. *Keywords: A Vocabulary of Society and Culture*. New York: Oxford University Press, 1976.

————. *Resources of Hope: Culture, Democracy, Socialism*. New York: Verso, 1989.

Wilson, Alexander. *The Culture of Nature: North American Landscapes from Disney to the Exxon Valdez*. Cambridge, Mass.: Blackwell, 1992.

Winthrop, John. "A Modell of Christian Charity." In *Early American Writing*. Edited by Giles Gunn, 108-12. New York: Penguin, 1994.

Wroble, David M. *The End of American Exceptionalism: Frontier Anxiety from the Old West to the New Deal*. Lawrence: University Press of Kansas, 1993.

Zahler, Helen S. *Eastern Workingmen and National Land Policy, 1829-1862*. New York: Columbia University Press, 1944.

Zimmerman, Michael. "The Role of Spiritual Discipline in Learning to Dwell on Earth." In *Dwelling, Place, and Environment: Towards a Phenomenology of Person and World*. Edited by David Seamon and Robert Mugerauer, 247-56. New York: Columbia University Press, 1989.

Zizek, Slavog. *The Plague of Fantasies*. New York: Verso, 1997.

Index

Alcatraz Island, 67-68
Amended Park Act, 21
American exceptionalism, 3-4, 8, 9,
    17, 42, 49, 76, 91, 113, 119n20
American Fur Company, 88
American Indian Movement, 76
American Industrial Association, 24
American Social Science Association,
    30
Arnold, Matthew, 17, 27-28; *Culture
    and Anarchy*, 26

Baker, Major Eugene, 87
Balibar, Etienne, 111-12
Banff National Park, 109
Bank of the United States, 18
Bannock, 94
barbarism, 42, 45, 47, 55-56, 58, 61,
    70, 102
Barlow, Capt. John W., 100-101
Bataille, Georges, 14
Baudet, Henri, 3
Beecher, Henry Ward, 100
Bellows, Henry, 43, 52, 54, 58
Bercovitch, Sacvan, 20-21
Berlant, Lauren, 9, 73-74
Beveridge, Charles, 25
Bhabha, Homi, 75
Biddle, Nicholas, 18
Bierstadt, Albert, 95
Blackfeet, 87-88, 89-90, 94, 95
Black Hills, 96
Blackmar, Elizabeth, 34, 37
Brace, Charles Loring, 44

Bunnell, Lafayette, *Discovery of the
    Yosemite and the Indian War of
    1851 Which Led to That Event*,
    50, 61
Burns, Ken, 95, 132n63
Bushnell, Horace, 53-54
Bryant, William Cullen, 21, 30

Carnegie, Andrew, 60
Catlin, George, 79-83, 84, 85, 93, 102;
    Beautiful Prarie Bluffs, 81
Central American Steamship Transit
    Company, 63
Central Pacific Railroad, 99
Central Park, 7, 11, 77, 103-04, 108-
    09; construction, 31; as cultural
    space, 27, 32; as exclusive 30; and
    municipal politics, 21-23; police,
    32; and surplus labor and capital,
    16, 20-21, 24; and visual or
    spatial rhetoric, 17, 39. *See also*
    Seneca Village
Chicago Columbian Exposition, 35
Chittenden, Hiram, 93-94, 101-02
civilization, 42; Olmsted's theorization
    of, 43-47, 53, 55-60, 63
Civil War, 1, 43, 58, 97
Clark, Malcolm, 88
class, conflict, 18, 31, 97; difference, 2,
    5, 7, 12, 35-37, 54, 76, 110; and
    race, 3, 7, 9, 53, 56; working
    class, 18, 47
coffeehouse, 54-55
Cole, Thomas, 79-80

About the Author

Stephen Germic is currently Visiting Assistant Professor of American Thought and Language at Michigan State University.